SPEED ON WHEELS

[Photo: *Courtesy Alfa-Romeo Car Club*

Sir Malcolm Campbell.

Speed on Wheels

by

SIR MALCOLM CAMPBELL

SAMPSON LOW, MARSTON & CO., LTD.
25 GILBERT STREET, LONDON, W.1

First published 1949

"The rush of air, the turning wheels,
The roar of metal steed,
Combined with grace of form provide
The Poetry of Speed."

This book is produced in complete conformity with the Authorised Economy Standards

MADE AND PRINTED IN GREAT BRITAIN BY PURNELL AND SONS, LTD.
PAULTON (SOMERSET) AND LONDON

FOREWORD

by

S. C. H. DAVIS

of *The Autocar*

MALCOLM CAMPBELL

NO DRIVER has attained to greater fame in the record world than Sir Malcolm Campbell. Probably no other man was so intensely anxious to succeed in this particular field of automobile sport. Even from the earliest days when Campbell, a small freckled boy, was at Hornbrook House School at Chislehurst, it was obvious that he had an almost overbearing desire to do something notable with any form of mechanical vehicle, the craze at that moment being for cycles. Borrowing a penny-farthing cycle belonging to a school friend, he even made efforts to master that entirely extraordinary and highly dangerous machine, but all the while it was obvious that he was thinking of record work of one kind or another in the future. Thus it was in no wise extraordinary that he appeared at Brooklands Track in the very early days and made a name for himself in races on that track before the 1914–18 war.

But it was in records that Campbell was outstanding. Beginning with the famous 12-cylinder

Sunbeam, 350 horsepower, which was built primarily for racing at Brooklands, year after year he produced a series of record cars, each year growing larger and faster, mostly with aircraft engines, and with them attacked and took the world's land speed record nine times, first at 146.16 miles an hour and lastly at 301.13 miles an hour. In the process he had a most interesting duel with Sir Henry Segrave, Segrave being the first man to attain to 200 miles an hour, Campbell the first to raise the record to 300.

Now the land speed record requires a special technique and quite definitely considerable courage, for the monstrous cars cannot be tested thoroughly before they are driven at maximum speed and so the driver has no certain knowledge that all will be well or even that the car will be completely stable. Moreover, the very nature of the record, the ultimate speed obtained, is governed by the tyres, for the car can drive no faster than the tyre designed will permit. It is only necessary to consider for one moment what all this means to realise what qualities the driver has to possess. He has, as Campbell had, a series of intense frustrations—days when the car is not right, when the timing turns out to be unsuitable, when the course chosen is in the end impossible for the speed, a fact only discovered when car, men and mechanics have been transported very many miles to the scene of operations. It is not wonderful, therefore, that Malcolm often had a very trying time, made worse by the fact that he was driven onwards always by the all-pervading, paramount desire to succeed. Had he not been, he would not have achieved success in the end. Even when he had attained to one ideal, 300 m.p.h., he did not relinquish his desire for further success and so turned his thoughts to the record on water, which is equivalent to the land speed record, and here again was successful. Only a few months before he died he was busy with a most unusual type of jet-engine-propelled racing boat with which he hoped that the record speed could be raised yet once more and with boats, as with cars, he had to fight and overcome innumerable difficulties.

It is just this lifelong fight to attain to an ideal which was the whole meaning of Sir Malcolm Campbell's career and which eventually led to his knighthood, and it is for this reason that his name will live for ever in the annals of motoring sport.

S.C.H.D.

PUBLISHERS' NOTE

The Publishers regret that Sir Malcolm Campbell did not see proofs of this book before his death, and therefore could not make any small revisions which he might have thought necessary, but the Publishers have checked the information in the book carefully to ensure accuracy.

S. L., M. & Co.

CONTENTS

LIST OF ILLUSTRATIONS

SPEED ON WHEELS

I

THE LURE OF SPEED

THE LURE of speed is an urge that most civilized human beings feel. I know that it has interested and fascinated me ever since the day—quite a number of years back now—when, mounted on a bicycle, I shot past two terrified old ladies down the steep slope of Bickley Hill in Kent at the rate of twenty-seven miles an hour. At least, that was the speed estimated by the constable who gave evidence at Bromley Police Court where I was charged the next day with having driven a bicycle to the danger of the public.

I was found guilty by the bench and fined thirty shillings. At the same time I was given a wigging and a warning, or should I say *words of advice.* "Malcolm Campbell," the presiding magistrate thundered, "you have endangered public life and property on a public highway. You drove this machine of yours at a totally unnecessary speed. If you come before us again, we will take a much more serious view of the matter. We hope this will be a lesson to you not to travel so fast in future."

This was a lesson I have never learnt. Since that day I have certainly managed to steer clear for the most part of speeding convictions, even though I have failed to take the magistrate's advice. He might just as well have told me, as a matter of fact, not to breathe or not to sleep as not to travel fast. Speed is in my very blood. I have raced and gone out for speed records because I loved it. I continue to do so because I love it. I will never give up until I have to. To me the competitive effort in trying to beat an existing record is the best of all sports. It is the most exhilarating of adventures.

The fascination of speed is something which I find it hard to describe. You either have this longing, this insatiable urge in your system—or you don't. Still, I hardly think my readers require many explanations about the joys and pleasures and thrills to be obtained from travelling faster and faster. It will be a sad day for Britain when its youth gives up the idea and desire for breaking records. But, somehow, I don't think that day has come yet.

To some people the lure of speed and the pleasure they derive from motoring consists in getting over the ground as quickly as possible, eating up miles and ever seeking the unreachable horizon. I have often attempted to analyse this craving for speed, and as I have had considerable experience in the matter I might reasonably be supposed to know the cause. I don't. I can only say, from instinctive experience, that this craving has kept on growing and growing, and, like some "diseases", has become stronger and stronger as time passes.

At the conclusion of my schooldays my father decided to send me to Germany to study. I went to Neu Brandenburg, and my bicycle accompanied me. It was a machine fitted with a freewheel, and this was a novelty at that time in this part of Germany. The inhabitants used to stand and stare when I coasted down the hills. I was always ready to race anything that I met on the road. This culminated in my entering against professionals on a bicycle track in the town. I borrowed a racing-machine, and secured third place. That was the first race I ever contested on wheels.

After eighteen months in Germany there followed a further six months at Caen in France. During a visit home I had told my father that I had no definite plans for my future occupation, although the new "horseless carriages" (as motor-cars were then termed) held some interest for me. He was not impressed at the suggestion and told me to learn French, and then come home with my mind made up. He was quite unsympathetic about my obsession for speed. "Forget those bicycles," he told me in no uncertain words, "and settle down to hard work. For heaven's sake think of what you are doing and your future. You don't seem to want to be anything, and it's not nearly good enough. If you can't make up your own mind I must do it for you."

My stay in France failed to bring about any decision which my father approved of. I had no desire to tie myself down to any sort of sedentary work. I told him this and added that I had nothing in mind except a strong inclination towards the motor business. He pooh-poohed this idea and thought he had solved the problem when he apprenticed me to a well-known firm at Lloyds. There I was obliged to work—work hard—and, in due course, became an underwriter. I also managed to save some money.

By this time my interest in speed had lured me from bicycles to motor-cycles. My first purchase was a second-hand Rex. It cost me fifteen pounds

—a lot of money to me at the time, for I was only eighteen years old. But it gave me a lot of fun, some adventures, and quite a number of crashes. By now I was regarded by my family and friends as little better than a lunatic. Still, this was the popular outlook at that time regarding those who were indulging in this new sport. Speed was fascinating me more and more. And when I finally ended up by hitting a brick wall on my machine and was picked up half-conscious, the inevitable moral was pointed out to me.

All the advice, all the warnings I was given, had, however, not the slightest effect on me. I followed up the Rex with more powerful machines, and had more crashes. I entered for the Motor Cycling Club long-distance reliability trial between London and Edinburgh, winning a gold medal. It was the first trophy which I had ever gained with a motor vehicle, and I was naturally very proud of it. To disprove the doubts of my friends who said my victory was a fluke I repeated my victory during the following two years, securing a further gold medal on each occasion.

It was a natural step to progress from motor-cycles to motor-cars. My first car was a Belgian make—a 7-h.p. Germain. Its top speed, when it was on its best behaviour, was about fifty miles an hour downhill. That was something terrific then. In fact, to many people not only the speed but the machine itself was regarded as a blasphemy. On several occasions while passing through Kentish villages I had stones, mud, fruit and eggs hurled at me. Horses shied at my approach, men swore, women screamed and even fainted, and children rushed away terrified as though the devil himself had made an appearance.

The pioneer in any new line of invention is seldom considered a hero, but in my search for speed I was not to be deterred. Mishap followed mishap—and I was perfectly happy. I hit a tramcar with this car and went over the steering-wheel into the tram-conductor's cab. On several occasions the machine caught fire. Tyres burst and wheels came off. I suppose it was all rather alarming. I certainly had a good initiation into my many coming bouts with the next world.

Flying, at this time in its pioneer stages, next attracted me. It almost seemed a safer pastime than motoring. A brief interlude in this sport, when I built my own machine, ended, however, disastrously. A sequence of smashes drained my financial resources, and I was obliged to give up. It was at the time a bitter disappointment. I returned to motor-cars and motor-racing.

I now bought a second-hand Darracq. It weighed just under a ton and it was capable of over 80 m.p.h. With this car I won my first race at Brooklands, achieving a speed of about 75 m.p.h.; I finished second in another race. A Peugot followed next, but as it brought me no luck I returned to a Darracq, this time a more powerful model than my first machine. It led me, however, into every kind of trouble (trouble and I are the oldest of friends!), and so I changed it for yet another and much faster Darracq.

The engine on my latest acquisition was really big, with cylinders over six inches in diameter, and it was capable of over 100 m.p.h.—a frightening speed in those days. This car was the first to be christened *Blue Bird.* I got the idea of the name from seeing Maeterlinck's play, *The Blue Bird,* which was then being performed in London. The new name was to change my racing luck. Right away I won two races with it. Since then I have given the same name to all my record-breaking cars.

Until the outbreak of war in 1914 I raced with a variety of cars. I had varying success and my usual crop of mishaps, some of them being miraculous escapes from death. It is a strange fact, however, that although I have seen innumerable crashes, spills, fires and deaths in motor-races, I find it difficult to remember much about them. They seem to have made no lasting impression. Perhaps it is just as well. It is not that I do not realize the danger of death or undervalue my own life. I am most meticulous, as are all record-breaking drivers, in attending to every detail concerning a racing-car and the conditions under which it has to travel. But, having done my best, I then believe in providence and luck.

Frankly, I am amazed at the luck which followed, not only me but many other drivers in those early days of motor-racing. By modern standards those pioneer cars were most dangerous. There was the Darracq with which I often raced. It had artillery wheels with wooden spokes, and these had shrunk in the rims. Rather than go to the expense of new wheels, I used to hose the wheels each time prior to a race, so that they fitted tightly while the machine was actually running.

I have spoken of the lure of speed being like some disease—an insatiable craving. When I drove my first 7-h.p. car I craved for a 10, and after that the speed obtained from a 15-h.p. engine seemed to offer every bliss in life. It was the same with speed: from 20 to 30, and from 30 to 40 m.p.h., and then on again, without limit. Perhaps it was because I took to racing that speed, pure and simple, appealed to me more than anything else. Driving a 40-h.p. car made me want a 70, not because I should stand a better chance of winning a particular race, but because I wanted to experience the sensation of travelling faster; and this desire still grips me, to travel yet faster and faster.

I have seen the same effects and longing for speed on various kinds of people whom one would not usually associate with this kind of pleasure. There is the quiet old man or the gentle, elderly lady whom one pictures as being quite content and happy in a comfortable arm-chair or pottering about in the garden; but put them behind the wheel of a powerful car and they seem to be possessed by the concentrated energy of a thousand fiends. Regardless of everybody and everything on the road, they race along with the sole idea of travelling quicker and quicker.

The old gentleman might well lack the courage to climb a high ladder on the side of his home, and the elderly lady might faint at the sight of a mouse, but both will drive a motor-car at great speed without turning a hair and without feeling that the performance is attendant with danger, either to themselves or to other users of the road.

The lure and intoxication of speed seems to lift them out of themselves and change them into new creatures. In time, of course, the feverish craving for speed may well depart, and a more moderate rate of progression takes its place; but the phase while it lasts is certainly curious.

The discovery that by using speed man could defeat the limitations imposed on his activities in other directions is as old as man himself, but progress in speed up to comparatively recent times has been very slow. Until the end of the eighteenth century, through thousands of years, speed was limited to the pace of the horse. Then, almost in a flash, with the discovery and invention of the steam-engine by Stephenson, there came a revolution in movement, in speed. In our own era we seem to have straddled history. The motor-car has been one of the chief instruments by which this has been achieved. The aeroplane has, also, made fantastic strides in the annihilation of distance. New York is to-day reached in less time from London by air than the time taken to journey to Edinburgh by any mode of transport only forty years ago.

It was just over fifty years ago, in fact, that we had in Britain an Act of Parliament known as the "Red Flag Act". This laid down that a mechanically propelled vehicle must be preceded along the highway by a person carrying a red flag. It was also laid down that such a "locomotive" was to be accompanied by at least three persons, and that its speed should not exceed four miles per hour on the open road or two miles per hour through built-up areas.

It was in 1896 that these penal laws against the use of motor-cars were repealed, although even this concession was accompanied by a further speed limit restriction of twelve miles per hour. It was, however, a great advance, and the day this new Act became law, November 14, was an important occasion in the history of speed. Since then it has been celebrated by motorists as "Emancipation Day". And it was from this date that the achievements which are described in this book have taken place.

From four miles per hour to 400! Along this road of progress are many milestones of records accomplished and won; and through all this fascinating story runs the incentive and spur—the lure to go on and on, faster and faster.

II

EARLY DAYS OF RECORD-BREAKING

THERE were no race tracks in the early days of motoring, but there were many road-races from one place to another, and sometimes back again. It was not very long before some of the cars were travelling very quickly indeed, and once motor-racing had really begun they improved in an extraordinary way. Very soon drivers began to try to find out just how fast they could cover a kilometre, the French unit of distance—and so the first speed records were set up. These began in 1898 when the Comte de Chasseloup-Laubat took an electrically-driven Jeantaud car over the kilometre distance at 39·2 m.p.h. This initial record took place at Achères, in France.

Less than a month later, Jenatzy, "The Red Devil", driving his own make of electrically-driven car, managed to raise the record by just over 2 m.p.h. During the following three months, the Comte and Jenatzy alternated in record-breaking. It was Jenatzy, however, who in April 1899 raised the speed to 65·79 m.p.h., and this was the first time that a speed of a mile a minute had been officially achieved by motor-car.

In the case of all these early records drivers only used to run in one direction. Subsequently a rule was introduced stating that no record would be recognized unless it was accomplished in both directions. The Americans, however, continued to run their attempts in one direction only, and consequently they were not recognized by the international body covering these events. From 1922 onwards, all official world's records have been made in both directions.

To-day most of us accept record-breaking as an ordinary and quite natural occurrence, but it was very different in the early days of motoring. At that time a considerable section of public opinion was definitely opposed even to the idea of motors, and the pioneers had no easy time, especially in Britain where hostility was extremely bitter, in carrying out their tests of speed.

The world's first competitive test of motor vehicles over the road was run between Paris and Rouen, and it was described as a "trial for carriages without horses". This eighty-mile test took place on June 22, 1894, only a few years after the first petrol-driven motor-car had made its appearance. This had been a little three-wheeled vehicle constructed by a German inventor, Carl Benz, having an engine of less than 1 h.p.

Everything at this time, it must be remembered, was in a very experimental stage. Entries for this first race included machines driven by petrol-motors, and others operated with steam-engines; there were a few electrically propelled vehicles, and some which were supposed to run on compressed air. A few designers even hoped to drive their cars by clockwork, while one or two employed hydraulic principles.

On the actual day of the test, however, only about twenty cars materialized at the starting-line. Some of these were steam-driven, the remainder running on petrol. All of them actually succeeded in making a start, the event being won by a De Dion Bouton steam-tractor, at an average speed of nearly 17 m.p.h. This car was followed by thirteen petrol-driven machines, while the rear was brought up by another steam-driven vehicle which reached Rouen about three hours after the winner had arrived, its average speed being barely 9 m.p.h.

The first machine (the De Dion Bouton) to reach the finishing-point was unfortunately disqualified. The reason being that the tractor had conveyed its passengers in an open-carriage trailer. This was against the rules which demanded that the engine should be in the carriage itself. So the honour of officially winning the first motor-race went to a petrol-driven Peugot car.

The excitement in France in connection with this race was great, the new vehicles being welcomed by the French populace with open arms. Enormous crowds gathered at the start and along the course, while the name of the car that won was flashed round the whole world. The French certainly grasped the importance of this new form of transportation, and their government gave the new industry every encouragement. For some years, therefore, French cars held the leading place.

The following year a much more ambitious race took place. This was held over the then enormous distance of nearly 750 miles—from Paris to Bordeaux and back. The start was at Versailles, and twenty-three vehicles presented themselves at the starting-point. Of these, nine completed the journey, eight of them being petrol-driven and one steam. This race was won by M. Levassor, driving a 4-h.p. Panhard, who accomplished the journey in forty-eight hours—a magnificent performance, considering the stage of development to which the motor vehicles had attained at that time. His speed averaged 14·9 m.p.h. The race proved a triumph for petrol-driven machines, because the only steam-car came in last, being forty-eight hours behind the winner.

During the next few years a number of long-distance races were held. It was not until 1902, however, that a British car and driver won an international event. This was a race from Paris to Innsbruck for the Gordon-Bennett cup, the winner being S. F. Edge on a Napier car. His average speed was 36·1 m.p.h. A month later another Englishman, Charles Jarrott, won the Circuit des Ardennes on a Panhard at an average speed of 54·3 m.p.h.

By this time really big cars were making their appearance. It was in 1903, however, that something occurred which was to change the whole course of motor-racing. The French ran the most dramatic event in all the history of speed. It was a contest, described by sensational newspapers as being the "Race to Death".

In this contest more than 200 cars of every description entered for a race from Paris to Madrid, a distance approaching 1,000 miles. The first car left Versailles at dawn on May 24. Among those which followed were many powerful machines that were unsafe at speed, while a large number of drivers naturally had little or no experience. The result was a series of terrifying accidents.

Some cars got out of hand and dashed into the crowds which gathered along the route. Many drivers were blinded because of the dust raised by the cars in front of them, and, in consequence, dashed off the road when they came to a turn. There were skids, crashes and accidents of every kind—so many, in fact, that the actual number of people hurt was never known.

Every few miles was the scene of a smash. Cars lay beside the road, some burned out, many overturned, and a great number abandoned. One machine had struck a dog, with the result that the car got out of control and hit a tree; the car was literally smashed to smithereens. A number of the contesting drivers were killed, and there were many deaths among the spectators.

Bordeaux was the halting-place for the first night of the race. It was also its conclusion. The French government acted in this matter without delay. They stopped the race forthwith, and the authorities took possession of all the racing-cars. Special trains were ordered which took the cars back to Paris. It was even forbidden to drive under power to the railway station, horses being provided to drag the vehicles there.

The fastest time from Paris to Bordeaux was made by Gabriel with his 70-h.p. Mors. Starting 168th, he came right past scores of cars, wrecks, and through blinding dust-clouds, averaging 65 m.p.h. This was the highest speed that had yet been attained in any long-distance race and it almost reached the record achieved by Jenatzy set up in 1899. Salleron on another Mors finished second; while Jarrott, the British driver, on a De Dietrich, was third.

Road-racing was dead after this great tragedy. It almost brought motor-racing to an end. It was certainly the last great road-race ever to be run on the classic French roads. Paris–Amsterdam, Paris–Berlin, Paris–Vienna—all were memories of the past, never again to be repeated. From that time on motor-racing took place over more or less circular routes. This enabled effective control to be established over traffic, spectators and competitors. This system is in operation at the present day, except in the case of the *Mille Miglia*, an annual affair held in Northern Italy.

During these early days of ever-increasing speeds on Continental roads, the position as far as Britain was concerned was in a completely different category: road-racing was entirely non-existent.

The great "Emancipation Day" certainly permitted motor-cars to use the roads of Britain, but the Act laid down certain restrictions which quite ruled out any idea that cars might speed. Motor-cars were allowed to travel at a speed not exceeding 12 m.p.h. In addition, they were forbidden to emit smoke!

November 14, 1896, was commemorated by a celebration run from London to Brighton, for which fifty-eight entries were received. Thirty-three competitors actually participated, and of these only thirteen arrived at Brighton. Perhaps the foggy, dull, wet, typical November day was responsible for the many failures on this important occasion.

During the next few years reliability trials and not speed races were the form of development followed in Britain. The most important of these was a 1,000-miles trial, organized by the Automobile Club and carried out in April 1900. There were eighty-three entries, of whom sixty-five actually started. Very few of the cars went through this trial without mishap, and only about half the starters completed the trials.

While British trials may not have had the spectacular appeal of Continental road-races, yet the method we were compelled to adopt through our restrictive laws did enable us to build up a reputation for reliability in performance as contrasted to mere speed.

It was this Thousand Miles Trial which, indeed, led to British manufacturers developing a racing type of car. In this development of a racing type of car, the British manufacturer was seriously handicapped by the absence of facilities for testing its speed and stamina. The possibility of organizing a race somewhere inside the United Kingdom had to be faced, and it was solved when a special Bill was passed permitting a road-race to be held in Ireland. This race took place in 1903. In 1904, the Isle of Man authorities also gave permission for a race to be held on their island.

The race in Ireland was a Gordon-Bennett event, brought about by the fact that S. F. Edge had won the race in the previous year. This entitled the winner to have the next race in his own country, which in this instance was Britain. The race itself was a very exciting affair, and was won by Jenatzy with a 60-h.p. Mercédès, his average speed for the total distance of 327 miles being 49·2 m.p.h.

Jenatzy, one of the greatest of old-time drivers, gained the nickname "Red Devil" by the daring character of his driving and by his auburn beard.

The Gordon-Bennett race was the first event that he had won, although he had been racing for some time, and he was typical of the courageous pioneers. It required real nerve to drive one of the very powerful, unwieldly, unstable cars of those days. In spite of their build they could achieve very high speeds, and did it over indifferent, winding and narrow roads.

The first Tourist Trophy Race was held in 1905, fifty-eight entries being received, among which were two steam-driven cars. In the race eighteen cars finished, the winner being J. S. Napier on an 18-h.p. Arrol-Johnson. As the intention of this contest was, however, to develop touring qualities in a car rather than mere speed, it did not go far to solve the problem of where cars could be raced.

Several schemes were proposed, for it was realized by many motor-car manufacturers that it was futile to expect this country to compete on equal terms with Continental rivals if high-speed testing could only be done by subterfuge.

Eventually, Mr. Locke-King, a pioneer in this direction, built a track at Brooklands, which was part of his estate. It was opened for use on June 17, 1907. It provided a place where motor-racing or high-speed trials could take place, and, although the track was deficient in certain respects, it nevertheless played a big part in the history not only of speed records but in the development of the motor industry.

At this time, 1907, the fastest speed ever achieved was that of a steam-driven car, which had run through a measured mile at Ormonde Beach—part of Daytona Beach, in Florida—at 121·5 m.p.h. This was an exceptional performance. Petrol-driven cars capable of 100 m.p.h. were then rare, so that when Brooklands was built it was not anticipated that machines would ever travel at speeds much higher than this. Many years have gone by since Brooklands was first opened, but the excellence of its design is shown by the fact that it has been lapped at a speed of over 140 m.p.h. Unfortunately Brooklands is no longer available. Some new testing-place for present-day British machines is badly required.

About a month after it was inaugurated, Brooklands enabled S. F. Edge to put up a twenty-four hours' record on a Napier at a speed of nearly 66 m.p.h. He covered 1,582 miles—the greatest distance at that time ever travelled by man in twenty-four hours.

It was not long before another track appeared, over in America. This was called the Indianapolis

[*Autocar* photograph

The first British-built Daimler Autocar.

[Photo: *St. John Nixon*

Hon. C. S. Rolls, founder of the House of Rolls-Royce, at the controls of his Peugeot.

Speedway, and although early difficulties were experienced, the course saw its first great race in 1911. The winning car averaged 75 m.p.h., which was a very good speed over a distance of 500 miles, because the course is oblong and has four difficult low-banked corners.

The rising speeds of cars show how machines were improving, while the early rivalry of steam-cars had long since been eliminated. Men now began to take the fullest advantage of motor-racing as an aid to progress. At first any car could enter a race, no matter what the size of its engine. As men found out how to build bigger and more powerful engines it became very necessary to introduce rules and regulations. Sometimes the amount of petrol that a car could use during an event was limited. This made entrants pay great attention to the quantity of fuel consumed by their power-units; it was no use making a car run very fast if it ran out of petrol before it could complete the course.

Sometimes limits of weight were enforced. This meant that a designer could put any size of engine into a car provided the whole machine did not exceed a certain maximum weight. In those days, naturally, the bigger the engine the greater the weight of the whole car. This rule had the automatic effect of making all engines in competing cars relatively the same size. Of course, if a designer was sufficiently ingenious to get more power from an engine as light of those of his competitors, then he gained an advantage, as he deserved.

There were other rules in which weight, fuel-consumption, and engine size were defined. Designers had thus to try and get the utmost power and speed from their machines, while complying with the conditions governing the race. Each of these regulations helped to improve motor-cars.

About this time events were organized such as the Coupé de l'Auto, which was open to cars of a limited engine capacity. Then there was the Grand Prix, designed to replace the Gordon-Bennett event. This race was truly international, attracting entries from half a dozen countries. These pre-war Grand Prix were epoch-making events, for they were the first real attempts to get down to power in relation to weight. The cars competing in them were the forerunners of the present-day light car.

The point which racing had now reached may be better appreciated if it is remembered that the car which won the first big road-race—the Paris-Bordeaux event—had a 4-h.p. engine, and won at

14·9 m.p.h. The car which won the first Grand Prix, in 1906, had 105 h.p. and a maximum speed of 90 m.p.h. This car was a Renault, and the size of its engine was 12,850 c.c.

These figures—12,850 cubic centimetres—represent the volume displaced by the pistons as they move up and down the cylinders. This method of calculation provides an easy means of appreciating the size of an engine. Its significance becomes apparent when the 1906 Grand Prix Renault is compared with the cars which competed in the 1914 Grand Prix.

In this latter contest the engines were limited to 4,500 c.c.—about one-third of the 1906 winner—yet they gave off something like 130 h.p., and the machines were capable of speeds as high as 110 m.p.h. From this it will be seen how much motor-cars had benefited from racing experience. Engines had become much smaller, yet they were more powerful, and the cars faster. Not only this, the engines used less petrol and oil, while the weights had considerably decreased. In spite of these improvements, however, the cars were still big and blundering, judged by modern standards. They required considerable skill in handling.

It was the 1912 French Grand Prix which brought about a tremendous effect on car design. All the cars competing were fitted with very large engines, having a rating of 59·6 h.p., except one which was a 30-h.p. Peugot. This engine was a comparatively small one, having a bore of 110 mm., and a 200-mm. stroke. It was a great race, and for many laps there was a terrific duel between Bruce Brown, an American, driving a big Mercédès, and Georges Boillot driving the Peugot. The Peugot eventually won the race, and this was really the first time that a small high-speed engine proved itself against the larger slow-running motor. From then onwards, makers realized the possibilities of the lighter car. It was, indeed, an epoch-making event.

I bought this Peugot myself after the First World War and raced it in many hill climbs and at Brooklands; and succeeded in putting up a World's Class Record with it in 1920.

Great preparations were made for the last pre-war Grand Prix, in 1914, which was held on a road circuit outside Lyons. The course measured about twenty-four miles to one lap, and had to be covered twenty times. It was triangular, with one long straight side, a short base, and another long side which held between seventy and eighty bends and turns within nine miles. The circuit was far more hazardous than any ever before employed for the race, and it was one to test not only the machines, but the skill of the men who drove them. The great importance of the race is shown by the fact that there were no less than forty-one machines at the start. They were sent off in pairs at thirty-second intervals, the first two getting away at eight o'clock in the morning.

In this race there were twelve French cars, nine from Italy, eight from Germany, five from Britain, two from Belgium, and two from Switzerland, and every machine had been prepared as carefully as possible. Right from the start the event developed into a fight between French and German cars, in the heat of which a Mercédès was wrecked on a turn, and a French machine dived off the road into a canal.

Drivers were slowed by the bends where the course twisted, but down the straight leg of the triangle they achieved amazing speeds, and Lautenschlager, on a Mercédès, was timed between 112 and 115 m.p.h. Soon he was duelling against a driver named Jules Goux, who handled a Peugot. For five laps these two hung together, then the Frenchman fell back, and finally the German cars established their supremacy, but only after a fight which aroused the crowd to high excitement as they watched the huge machines thunder past.

Lautenschlager won, his speed being 65·8 m.p.h., two other Mercédès came in second and third, and Goux was fourth, while the fifth place was taken by a British car—a Sunbeam driven by K. Lee Guiness.

Within a month after the dust of the race had died down the First World War broke out, and motor-racing came to an end for more than five years. Most of the men who had designed those old racing-machines now turned their attention to building aero engines, and from these activities they learned so much that when, after the war, they began to build racing-machines again the new cars were entirely different from those which had been the fastest in the world in 1914.

The era I have described in this chapter might well be regarded now as "the good old days". At the start of this twenty-year period to be a motorist was equivalent to being an object of ridicule, scorn and abuse. By 1914 this outlook had been lived down. The motor vehicle had by then become a power in the land, its utility proved and permanence assured. Originally a plaything of the rich, it had become a necessity for the multitude, and an important factor in the lives of the people.

From the racing point of view I look back on those early days with nostalgia. Motor-cars certainly then had most peculiar vagaries, but one felt all the time the thrill and great expectations of the pioneer, with vast possibilities opening before one. There was the indescribable excitement that comes to the explorer in search of his goal.

Much joy came, too, from the good fellowship of those who engaged in early racing contests. They were the best of sportsmen. My mind goes back over the many happy incidents of the past, and I feel I should be leaving a sorry blank were I not to pay tribute to those good fellows and good comrades, some of my erstwhile rivals in so many motor-races.

My pleasure in these memories of the past is marred by the thought of the old faces that have now disappeared. Still, when I do look back on the early days, so do the names of Boillot, Goux, Nazzaro, Charles Jarrott, Edge, Algy and K. Lee Guiness, to mention only a few, bring back visions of struggle and happy meetings.

Before I conclude the story, brief though it has necessarily been, of those pioneer days, I would like to describe a personal experience with the machine which was the first *Blue Bird*. This particular car, a Darracq, had been built for an important race in 1909—the Vanderbilt cup, held in the United States. Its engine was very powerful (165 mm. bore and 140 mm. stroke), and the car was capable of over 100 m.p.h.

I bought it from Darracq in 1911 and drove it down to Brooklands, where, after we tuned the engine, it won many races. On August Bank Holiday, 1912, I entered it for two races on that day. This old car had canvas tyres, and before an event it was necessary to soak the wheels in water in order to make the wooden spokes swell and fit tightly into the rims.

During the first race my car came round on its last lap, travelling at over 100 m.p.h. and gaining rapidly on the three machines ahead of me, with every chance of overtaking them. As we approached a spot where the track forked into the finishing straight a front tyre burst. The car immediately lurched outward into a hundred-mile-per-hour skid. I managed to straighten out of this skid, only to have the wheel which had the burst tyre hit a low concrete kerb at the edge of the track. The wooden wheel was smashed instantly and completely, while the tyre shot off, narrowly missing an official who was standing behind the nearby railings. The rim actually hit these railings, badly smashing them, while broken spokes flew high into the air.

What seemed like an eternity, but was in reality a fraction of a second later, the rear wheel on the same side of the car also hit the kerb. This wheel too was shattered, making the car lurch over at a dangerous angle, for I had now lost both wheels on the off-side. It was, of course, impossible for me to steer the machine, but I had managed to lock the steering over to the near-side. This fortunately kept it on a fairly straight course, even though it was really skidding sideways right down the length of the finishing straight on its hubs. Gradually it slowed down, coming to a stop just a few inches from some railings behind which spectators were massed. They were all spellbound and seemed unable to move from this awe-inspiring spectacle.

That old car—a real museum-piece to-day—with its wooden wheels and loose spokes, its canvas tyres and heavy steering, was the sort of machine in which the pioneers of motoring used to race. A modern driver would hardly dare attempt in such a machine the speeds those old-timers used to achieve. I should mention, however, that by 1914 the cars competing in the Grand Prix showed considerable improvements on this old Darracq, and most of them had wire-spoked wheels and far better tyres.

III

THREE MILES A MINUTE

DURING the years immediately following the First World War motor-car designers were able, largely as a result of the knowledge and experience they had gained in the building of aeroplane engines, to effect such great improvements in the performance of racing-cars that a fresh start was possible in the attainment of speed records. It is because of these developments that the remarkable heights reached to-day have been rendered feasible.

I have related in the last chapter how Comte de Chasseloup-Laubat set up the first official speed record, in 1898, of 39·2 m.p.h. This was with an electrically-driven car. And I have also told how this record was raised within the short period of four months to above 60 m.p.h. (It is amusing to think that fifty years before this mile-a-minute record was established learned men had declared that any person attempting to travel at such a speed would find their blood congeal and their heart stop—death, in fact. The speed of railways had, in the interval, already disproved this strange theory.)

Step by step the speed record was raised. It was not, however, until five years later, in 1904, that it attained 100 m.p.h. This feat was accomplished by a French driver, Rigolly, driving a Gobron-Brillié, its motive power being alcohol. This performance by the first man to travel by car at over a hundred miles per hour—his official time over the flying kilometre was 103·56 m.p.h—was carried out at Ostend, in Belgium. At that time there was no official mile record recognized. It was not until 1909 that the first British Mile Record was accepted by the Royal Automobile Club. This was achieved by V. Hemery driving a Benz at 115·923 m.p.h., but it was not a world record.

A couple of years elapsed before a steam-powered machine, a Stanley, driven by Marriott at Ormonde in Florida made an official record of 121·52 m.p.h.—over two miles a minute. This took place in January 1906. The record which it set up is important, because the best speed that a petrol-driven car had achieved up to this time was 109·6 m.p.h. Despite this achievement, however, it was considered then that steam-powered machines were not very practical. In fact, after this performance the fight for the land-speed record rested entirely between petrol-driven cars.

In 1908 a huge Fiat, which was nicknamed *Mephistopheles*, beat the steam-car's record by a tiny increase, recording 121·64 m.p.h. Six years later, in the summer of 1914, L. G. Hornstead, driving a Benz, raised the record to 124·10 m.p.h. There then followed a long gap of seven years, due to the war, during which no attempts could be made. It was not until 1921 that K. Lee Guiness started a new and very thrilling battle for world honours. His giant machine was a 350-h.p. Sunbeam, and it had a twelve-cylinder engine with a capacity of over 18,000 c.c. With this car Lee Guiness made an attack on the record at Brooklands, where he covered the measured mile at a speed of close on 129 m.p.h., beating handsomely anything that had been done before. Soon after I managed to borrow this car, and experienced both the great thrill of high speed—or what seemed high speed in those days—and something of its disappointments.

Before describing my own first attempts on the world's speed record, I would like, briefly, to mention the developments that took place in great road-races between the two wars. The French

Grand Prix gave place to a race known as the Grand Prix de l'Automobile Club de France. In this race the engine-size of cars was limited, and it was soon discovered that building special machines for this type of event was a very costly matter.

Designers could now get great power from small engines, but this involved using very expensive metals. Consequently, few manufacturers were prepared to build special racing-cars. As a result Grand Prix racing began to die out. In its place organizers of events hit on the plan of arranging races similar to the Tourist Trophy, in which the entered cars were production "sports models".

It was thus easy for manufacturers to compete in these races. All they had to do was to take one of their normal sports-cars and tune it up. The result was to produce very popular events like the Grand Prix d'Endurance at Le Mans, where cars ran ceaselessly for twenty-four hours. Brooklands saw similar races, and the Italians arranged a 1,000-mile event over the northern part of their country, calling it the *Mille Miglia*.

As the various countries recovered from the effects of war, and as competing cars still further improved, there came a revival of Grand Prix racing. Regulations were framed to govern it, and these settled for each three years the formula under which cars could race. This gave manufacturers a chance to build true racing-cars again, knowing that it would be at least three years before they became out-of-date.

All over Europe Grand Prix events revived. Soon nearly every country had its own Grand Prix, rivalling the famous event which the French had been the first to organize. Even Great Britain organized a Grand Prix, and held it for two consecutive years at Brooklands.

By the end of 1933 Grand Prix cars were achieving speeds of over 150 m.p.h., and the machines employed were directly developed from those which had appeared just after the war. They were very light in weight, equipped with engines tuned to give maximum power, low-built, and responsive—veritable greyhounds of speed compared with the bellowing monsters that had run in 1914.

They had progressed very steadily, but now there came a tremendous leap forward. For a long time experts had been of the opinion that cars would be safer if each wheel was supported by springs which worked independently, and this idea was developed by German designers. Into the lists of Grand Prix racing they sent a new type of

Mercédès and an altogether new car known as Auto-Union.

During preliminary trials these machines showed that they were capable of amazing speeds; first 180 m.p.h., then 190 m.p.h., and then one of them achieved 199 m.p.h. Once they settled down to racing it became evident that they outclassed the existing Grand Prix design.

The result of this was that all manufacturers interested in racing also studied the question of independent springing. An Alfa-Romeo was produced—an Italian car—and during a record attempt this machine beat the highest speed yet achieved by the Germans, and reached a new peak of over 200 m.p.h. This car was, of course, specially prepared for the effort, but the majority of the machines which are independently sprung can all do about 180 m.p.h. on the road.

Many years have gone by since the first motor-race was held, and many, too, since the giants of old fought out the 1914 Grand Prix and held the spectators breathless as their machines touched over 100 m.p.h. along the straight. Just as those cars were an improvement on the first racing-machines, in the same measure are modern cars a still further improvement.

The 1914 models, we have seen, had about

4,500-c.c. engines, did about 110 m.p.h., and gave off 130 h.p. These new Grand Prix racing-cars also had engines of about 4,500 c.c., but they could do at least 180 m.p.h., and they gave off something like double the horse-power.

There was one event of great importance which took place in the 1920 Grand Prix, proving the value of racing in design. Ballot fitted up one of his racing-cars that was competing in this event with front-wheel brakes, for he found in practice that he saved a few seconds per lap with this new form of braking. In consequence this car won that race. It was from then onwards that manufacturers realized the value of front-wheel braking.

What the racing-cars of the future will be like it is impossible to say. It is unlikely that they will be capable of much more than 200 m.p.h., because this seems to be the limit of useful road-speed, even for very skilled drivers. It is probable that they will have still smaller engines, which means that they will be more efficient than the highly effective racing-cars that clever designers and courageous drivers have given us to-day.

. . . . .

I will now return to my early experiences with the Sunbeam. I used this car for an attack on the

[*Autocar* photograph

In the Paris–Marseilles contest, this Panhard-Levassor came second.

[Photo: *St. John Nixon*

1894 Panhard-Levassor, 2-cylinder V engine, single chain drive from inside counter shaft, wholly exposed gear.

[Photo: *St. John Nixon*

This is the rear view of the first Benz, built in 1884–5.

[Photo: *St. John Nixon*

A petrol driven car made by the late J. H. Knight of Farnham in 1895.

[Photo: *St. John Nixon*

June 1895. This was the second petrol driven car in England.

[Photo: *St. John Nixon*

This weird-looking machine is a Lanchester, built in 1896. It was the first British-built 4 wheeled petrol car.

record during trials at Saltburn Sands, on the coast of Yorkshire, and made several runs, the fastest being at about 138 m.p.h., while I know that the car actually went well above 140 m.p.h.

It was a fine, sunny day on which I made this speed; the sand was smooth and hard, and a crowd of several thousands lined the beach. The outward run was excellent, completely free from trouble.

On the return journey, travelling at well over two miles a minute, I suddenly saw a dog walking across the track. Swiftly I calculated our respective speeds. If the dog kept on walking I would just be able to miss him. If the dog turned back there would be the most unholy crash. Ten pounds of dog hit at the rate of a hundred and thirty-five miles an hour is enough to wreck most racing-cars. Fortunately the dog kept on walking. The car missed him by less than six feet. The last heard of that dog was that he had beaten the canine record for the hundred yards, and was still going strong into the North Sea!

Unfortunately, although this effort beat the previous record it did not establish an official record, for the governing authorities would not recognize it; I had been timed by stop-watches, but they now demanded much more reliable and efficient checks by electric timing tapes.

The machine, of course, actually held the world's land-speed record, because of what Lee Guiness had done at Brooklands. His effort was the last occasion on which such a record was set up on a track. In order to go through the mile at Brooklands he had been obliged to dive off the banking to the railway straight, and race on to the banking again at the far end, while, of course, he had not enjoyed an absolutely straight run. Still further, the nature of the track was such that he had never been able to work the car up to its absolutely maximum speed before entering the measured distance.

Soon after, I bought this car and decided to make world records a hobby. I entered it for the International Speed Trials which were to be held at Fanoe in Denmark, in June 1923.

It was the first time since the war that Britain had been represented at international speed trials on the Continent. My Sunbeam was the only British entry, but Germans, Frenchmen, Italians, Austrians and Danes had all entered cars.

From the start I was beset with difficulties. There was delay in delivering the car to me at my home which was in Surrey. When I came to tune it up, I discovered that two of its gears were worn out, hopeless, and fit for nothing. Without them she was, of course, worse than useless.

By a superhuman effort the Sunbeam Company managed to make new gears. To do this they had cut them out of a solid block of special steel. This steel had to be obtained from Vickers. Working day and night, the job was completed—only just in the nick of time. With my mechanics I was due to leave from Liverpool Street Station by the 2.30 train on the Monday. When I got to the station there was no sign of the gears, and it was only just a minute or two before the train was due to leave that the Sunbeam mechanic broke through the barrier and came running up the platform. He was out of breath and streaming with perspiration —but he gave me a heavy parcel, which contained the precious gears.

During the record attempts at Fanoe the Sunbeam actually did touch 150 m.p.h.—travelling flat out, with sand flying and the wind screaming—while its average pace through the measured mile proved to be 146·4 m.p.h. on one run. The return mile was slower, owing to the high wind, and the mean speed of the double run was 137·72 m.p.h., beating the existing record by a handsome margin.

This was the first and only time in my life when I ever had a sensation of real speed. Even at Daytona in 1931, when I travelled a full hundred miles faster, I had nothing like the sensation of speed which I experienced over the sands at Fanoe.

When we left Denmark I thought that we really had taken the record, but fate again stepped in unkindly. No risks had been taken with stop-watches this time. The electrical timing apparatus used had been tested and found accurate. It met with the approval of the Danish authorities who had organized the trials. But when the record came up for confirmation by the Central International body which confirms all the world land-speed records, it was announced that the timing apparatus used was not of a type approved by that official body.

Once again a record, carefully worked for, hardly won, costing, in its infinite details of preparation, a large sum of my own money, had been disallowed. Still, the only thing to do was to try again. In the meantime, however, *Mephistopheles* had reappeared. This old car was now in the hands of E. A. D. Eldridge, a well-known driver, who took it over to France. Here the machine provided a tremendous spectacle when he made an attempt on the record along a perfectly straight stretch of road. Eldridge registered a speed of over 148 m.p.h., but he had a disappointment, because it was a regulation that all machines for the land-speed record had to be fitted with a reverse gear and there was not one on his car.

After fitting the necessary gear, he tried again. After a good many troubles he got the big Fiat full out and quite thought he had broken the record, only to find this time that somebody had stepped on one of the electrical timing strips used to check the machine's speed, spoiling his effort. When everything was ready for another attempt the timing gear itself failed, and he was obliged to give up.

. . . . .

In spite of all the difficulties and disappointments which seemed to come my way, I was more than ever determined to get the official world record. I was also determined at the same time to be the first man to travel at a hundred and fifty miles an hour, just as later I set my heart on being the first man to do three hundred miles an hour on land.

The big Sunbeam and the old Fiat had shown that 150 m.p.h. was quite possible. Once again I took the car over to Fanoe. This time I arranged with the R.A.C. to take their own official timing apparatus in order to avoid the trouble I had experienced previously.

This time, however, other troubles turned up.

The climatic conditions were terrible: gales and high seas. The beach was in a terrible condition, and it was just about as dangerous as any sand track could be. To try and drive over it at high speed would have been suicide. When the weather improved, I then made an attempt on the record, but still without success, because the machine shed its tyres, and, eventually, I had to give up. This was most unfortunate, for the car itself was in really fine condition; it gathered speed magnificently and entered the mile, on its first attempt on the record, at well above 140 m.p.h., still accelerating. I felt the machine start to "crab", as it always did, and it was as I began to bring it straight that both tyres were torn from the rear wheels.

They left the rim almost simultaneously. The off-side one flew clear, but the other slipped inside its wheel, crashing against the body and just missing my left elbow, which jutted over the side of the cockpit. The tyre then jammed against the brake-arm, ramming on the brakes.

Instantly the car pitched into a 140-m.p.h. skid, but by good luck it was this skid which threw the jammed tyre clear. It flew away from the wheel in one gigantic leap, releasing the brake and overtaking the off-side tyre.

All this happened in the fraction of a second and, with the brakes off, I was able to straighten out the car. While I did so, I could see both tyres rolling ahead, travelling almost side by side and looking like great hoops as they plunged towards the sea. The soft sand near the water's edge diverted them, and with the Sunbeam still skidding and sliding, the tyres shot across the front of the car in the direction of the sand dunes. When they hit rough ground they jumped high into the air again and again, finally vanishing from sight and eventually coming to rest without doing any damage.

By that time I had the car under control and slowing down. I drove on to the depot which the mechanics had established, and during that short journey I had plenty of time to appreciate the narrowness of my escape. If the tyre had caught my arm I should have been left with the task of trying to straighten the machine one-handed, which at that speed would have been impossible. Luckily, it did not hit me, and another piece of good fortune lay in the streamline fairing formed by the discs where they shrouded the brake-drums. This projection had prevented the tyre locking the brake-arm completely; had it been able to do so, the Sunbeam must have spun in circles, running into soft sand and turning over.

The car itself, strange to relate, had not suffered at all, and required only a wheel change before we could try for the record again, but we decided to use different tyres. Those which had been thrown off were known as "beaded edge", and were held on to the wheel by security bolts; these bolts were fitted in order to prevent the tyre creeping around the wheel-rim and tearing out the valve to the inner tube. If that happened, the tube would deflate, and the tyre would fly off the wheel. I had lost the two rear tyres because, owing to the way in which the car "crabbed", a side-strain was set up, which threw off the tyres.

A second type of tyre existed, known as "straight-sided", and we had brought over a set, with their attendant wheels. These tyres could not be thrown off, but they could creep and pull out the valve. We fitted two of them to the rear of the car, but it seemed safe to leave the beaded-edge tyres on the front wheels, because they were not subjected to the same strain. While Leech and Villa, my two mechanics, were working on this, I spoke to the officials asking them to have the crowd moved further back. I had previously complained about this matter and also suggested that the timing-box should be set in a less dangerous position.

If the rear tyres had come off where the spectators lined the course, some of the people must inevitably have been killed. I had never seen tyres leave a car in the impressive way these two had flown from the Sunbeam; the velocity behind them had been very great indeed, while the tyres themselves were heavy. I told the officials this, but they felt certain no real danger existed, when I remarked that if anything did happen, the blame must rest with them. All I could do was to make ready for another run.

We took the Sunbeam back to the starting-point, which was indicated by tall, slender poles carrying flags; quite a crowd had gathered here now, watching while the engine was warmed up. With everything in good trim, I sent the machine away and it gathered speed magnificently, travelling at 100 m.p.h when I changed into top gear. Still accelerating, the car roared towards the start of the measured mile, down the length of which more thin flag-staffs were set, with ranks of spectators showing darkly between them, standing on either side of the cleared course.

Near the peak of the Sunbeam's speed, the car tried to "crab", and I had as much as I could do to keep it straight. Aiming the machine along the narrow course was very like entering a narrow road, and when I sent it squarely across the centre of the timing tapes, I was wedged down in the cockpit, with my foot rammed hard on the throttle pedal so that it could not be shaken by the bumps. The car was doing 140 m.p.h. then, increasing its speed as it dashed along the gradually thickening spectators on one side.

I picked out the banner at the end of the mile, whipping under the steady wind, and saw a big crowd just before the timing-box. I was two hundred yards short of this, travelling at a genuine 150 m.p.h., when the car suddenly lurched, its tail swinging outwards so that the machine headed straight towards the crowd, exactly as though some enormous force was thrusting it round.

For a moment I imagined that the steering gear had broken, then, as I instinctively tried to correct the skid, I saw something rolling and leaping beside the car. The machine was catching up and passing the blurred shape, and I thought it was the off-side front wheel. I expected the Sunbeam to get completely out of hand, and it seemed inevitable that it must crash into the timing-box. I was using all the strength I had in an effort to wrench the machine back on to its course, easing the throttle at the same time, and the car skidded for a hundred yards before I was able to bring it straight, when it crossed the timing tape safely and ran clear of the crowds.

It skidded again, then slowing down, I saw that it was not a wheel which had gone; the off-side front tyre had flown off. As I brought the machine to a stop, a crowd which waited at the end of the cleared course came running towards me, cheering and waving; they knew that something had happened, and were expressing relief, as people do when they see disaster averted. But I knew that the tyre must have been thrown into the packed spectators, and it seemed certain that some damage had been done.

Looking back, I saw people swarming across the course at the end of the measured mile, and it was not long before I learned that the tyre had struck a boy standing near the timing-box. The boy was severely injured, and the mishap meant that my worst fears had been realized. Further record attempts were cancelled immediately, and the unfortunate boy lived only a short while.

We took the car back to the shed, all of us very upset at what had occurred. Later on, I learned that the car had been timed through the mile at 139·81 m.p.h., in spite of the lost tyre; the record would have been sure if I had made a reverse run, although that was out of the question.

Presently I was shown two unusual photographs of the incident; one had been taken by a photographer kneeling on the sand, who had clicked his camera just as the car passed him. Until he developed his negative, he did not know that he had actually secured a picture of the car and of the tyre flying from it. The other photograph had been taken by a man standing a few yards from the timing tape; this picture showed the first photographer on the sand and the tyre spinning away from the car, while it also revealed the boy who was hit the fraction of a second later, just on the corner of the timing-box. The crowd remained immobile, with the exception of one man who stood near the boy. He had his arms upraised and was running from the tyre.

An inquiry followed the accident; the investigation lasted a long time, and it was something of an ordeal. It was not that I expected to be blamed, but I could appreciate the feelings of the boy's parents and felt inexpressibly sorry. The accident affected me all the more when I realized that, had the officials taken my advice, it would never have occurred. To have been the means of killing the little fellow was too terrible for words.

I believe we were all under some sort of arrest, and we were not allowed to leave the island until after the inquest, but the investigation resulted in complete exoneration for myself and my mechanics, after which we packed up and came home again. It took me a long time to forget the tragedy. After this accident, the Danish authorities stopped all further racing in Denmark.

For the fourth time I had attempted to break the record, and still again I had failed. The circumstances surrounding the effort certainly became a warning to all promoters of similar events, while the tyre trouble made it quite clear that, for high-speed work, a new type of tyre should be used.

Dunlops began a thorough investigation of the whole tyre question, because they saw far enough ahead to realize that speeds would become still higher; finally, they evolved an altogether different type of rim and tyre, which eliminated the faults even of the straight-sided type. But for what happened at Fanoe, their investigations might have been postponed for some time; coming when it did, the work achieved by Dunlops was a great contribution to safety, not only to record attempts, but to normal motoring, and in consequence was eventually used on all touring-cars.

Two months later I took this same car to the Pendine Sands on the west coast of Wales. It looked as though my ill-luck was going to be repeated. The weather was vile, the sands were sodden, it was blowing a gale and the sky was full of driving masses of grey clouds. I decided, however, to make the attempt. The timing apparatus was checked and made ready—then I started off.

Patches of soft sand still impeded the machine. I could feel it slow, then accelerate again when it reached a harder surface. I made four runs in each direction, and each run appeared to be faster than the last, but every time I drove into soft sand I had to guard against skidding, and suffered from much wheel spin, so that I was kept busy. It was most exhausting. I had to grip the steering-wheel very tightly—a definite physical strain. There was also the mental strain of remaining constantly alert in order to prevent the machine running out of control.

Feeling more than a little tired, I finally ran the big car back to the finishing post, and then learnt that the average speed of our two fastest runs was 146·16 m.p.h.—a new world's record.

So far so good, but the record was not likely to stand for long. I naturally wanted to hold it. Also, it seemed very much worthwhile to try and gain the honour of being the first man to reach 150 m.p.h., which was only a little faster than the big Sunbeam had already done. There seemed to be a good deal of competition for this honour. New competitors and new cars were looming up on every side. Over in Paris an Italian engineer, Moglia, was actually constructing a car, which was being financed by an Egyptian prince. The car was given the name of *Djelmo*; it had a 400-h.p. engine, and was very beautifully streamlined. They expected that the car would achieve what was then regarded as the phenomenal speed of 180 m.p.h.

The Sunbeam firm was also building a special car for Sir Henry Segrave, while Parry Thomas was busy building his enormous 500-h.p. Liberty-engined *Babs*, the car which brought him so much honour before it killed him.

Under the circumstances I decided that I must get a new car, designed on lines which would place it far ahead of the other competitors. I approached several motor manufacturers and tried to interest them, but without success. I did not allow this, however, to discourage me, and I decided to build my own motor-car. This special car was to have a 450-h.p. Napier-Lion engine, and was to be designed for a maximum speed of 180 m.p.h. As this machine would have to be constructed throughout by hand it was obvious that it would take a long time to build, but details were arranged, and the preliminary work commenced.

By the summer of 1925 I realized that this new car would not be finished for at least another year, so I decided to make one more effort with the 350-h.p. Sunbeam, and find out if this machine could be made to travel through the measured mile at 150 m.p.h. Certain improvements and alterations were made, and I took the machine to Pendine in July 1925.

Sands, weather, course and car were all alike ideal, and, for probably the first important occasion in my life, everything went off without a hitch. I knew that the speed I wanted to reach was not much faster than I had travelled before, but I also knew that this little extra would require quite considerable effort to achieve. Once the car was under way I braced myself hard in the driving seat, so that my foot was jammed flat against the throttle pedal and could not be shaken off by any bumps.

With the car travelling flat out, everything—flags, dunes, scattered spectators, and the beach itself—appeared to rush to meet me. The pressure of the wind about my head was so great that the air felt very much like water. The car threw spray and sand far and wide, and it travelled amazingly well. Its fastest speed was 152·8 m.p.h., and we actually set up a new world's record with 150·7 m.p.h.

[Photo: *St. John Nixon*

The first Wolseley car was built between 1895 and '96.

[*Autocar* photograph

What "The winner" of the 1900's looked like—Charron's 24-h.p. Panhard.

through the measured mile. This, I felt, was indeed a milestone in the history of motor-racing.

Consider the progress in speed. Since 1922, and in the course of three years, land speed had been lifted in the official records from 129 m.p.h. to 150 m.p.h., and all by this big Sunbeam car. This new record created a good deal of public interest, and everyone wanted to know whether cars could be made very much faster.

Of course, this kind of thing had the effect of stimulating the drivers who had contemplated attacking the record. The Sunbeam firm grew very busy over their new car for Segrave, while Parry Thomas began to tune up his really big car, *Babs*, which had a 27,059-c.c. engine. And all this, it must be borne in mind, was happening in 1925.

So far these attempts on the world's record had all been made with cars that had enormous engines, but the Sunbeam firm now approached matters from a new angle. They gave their car an engine which was not a quarter the size of that in the 350-h.p. Sunbeam. Its size was actually only 3,977 c.c., but it was fitted with a supercharger, and actually gave off 300 h.p. With this car Segrave went to Southport sands, and pushed up the record to 152·3 m.p.h. (although this was effected over a kilometre course only, so that my previous figure held good for the mile). At this time, while we were working hard on my new machine Parry Thomas suddenly appeared on the beach at Pendine with his new *Babs,* all ready to attack Segrave's figure.

It is necessary to explain that up to this point these attempts had never been organized in any special way. What one did was to turn up with the car, see that everything about the course was in order—that it was marked out as well as possible, and that the time-keepers were on the job—and them simply drive the car. Obviously the work could be materially aided if everything was planned in advance, and the attempt which Parry Thomas now made was arranged after full attention had been paid to earlier experiences.

He secured something like fifty willing helpers, equipped with motor-cycles and cars. There were police to keep the crowd off the course—which was necessary because many hundreds of spectators came to watch, a thing that had never happened before. There was also a doctor in attendance, and officials saw to it that the course was marked out very efficiently, with the start and finish of the measured mile definitely indicated. Thomas's efforts occupied two days, and ended when the land-speed record took one magnificent jump from

Segrave's 152·3 m.p.h. to the figure of 170·6 m.p.h. Over one particular run the machine had actually registered 172 m.p.h. All of which meant that Thomas had raised the record by almost a solid 20 m.p.h.

It was a wonderful achievement, and it came at a time when our new car was nearing completion. And as an indication of the disappointments and heartbreak that these record attempts can bring stands the situation with which we were faced. My new car—which we intended to call *Blue Bird*, continuing the name given to other machines which I had raced—was still not ready; it had been designed to travel at a maximum speed of 180 m.p.h.—only 10 m.p.h. faster than Thomas had already travelled. Moreover, Thomas said that his *Babs* was quite capable of 180 m.p.h., and that he meant to try and reach this speed as soon as he had returned his machine—which made our *Blue Bird* almost useless for the record before the car had as much as turned a wheel. Even if we did get the car running well the best of which it was capable would be only a little in excess of the new speed. Beyond all this, Segrave wanted to get the record back, and the Sunbeam firm were already planning another car for him. This machine was not to aim at 180 m.p.h., or 190 m.p.h., but at nothing less than the astonishing figure of 200 m.p.h.

There were many people ready to say that 200 m.p.h. was impossible. They said that such a speed would tear up the ground over which the car itself ran, and that no driver would be able to hold the machine. But when clever and experienced engineers set such a pace as their aim one may be sure that they will not be very far out in their calculations.

The only thing for us to do with *Blue Bird* was to complete the machine as rapidly as possible and attack the record before it was lifted to a figure beyond the car's capabilities. It was finally made ready, and was rushed off to Pendine for an effort which began just after New Year's Day 1927. But once more the bogy of ill-luck which has so often dogged my footsteps pursued me.

No sooner had we arrived than we discovered a defect in the gear-box. So back the car had to go to Surrey on a lorry, a return journey of nearly 500 miles.

On its return to Pendine more trouble developed, and so home she came again once more. Finally, in February, I took the car out on the sands and she appeared to be all right. But if the car was ready, the beach was not fit to drive on. Gales were blowing, the days were short, the tides were running high, piling wreckage all along the beach, while the sands were so choked with water that even an ordinary touring-car sank up to its axles if it was allowed to stand still for a few minutes.

Day after day I tried for the record. Day after day I had to give it up. But on firm stretches of sand *Blue Bird* behaved splendidly, and over one run I actually touched 171·3 m.p.h. We tried again, and this time I came into the mile at fully 170 m.p.h., when the car ran into another of those soft, wet patches of sand. Immediately it skidded sideways and slid off the course, travelling like that for about half a mile, chopping down one of the marker flagposts as it went. Fortunately I kept control, but the mishap ruined the effort.

For the next two weeks the state of the tide would not allow any further attempts. Then the weather became vile. We had to use a plough to cut furrows along the beach to drain the water away and secure something like a dry course when the tide was out. At last a day came when the conditions improved. By this time I almost felt desperate as I started off.

The car accelerated marvellously. I soon knew that I was certainly travelling far faster than I had ever gone before. The wind pressure was tremendous, and the noise of the wind drowned all sound from the car itself. The sensation of speed was exhilarating, and during a part of that run *Blue Bird* was actually travelling at 184 m.p.h. —just over three miles a minute. The speed recorded over the measured distance, however, was 179 m.p.h. I still had the return trip to make to achieve the record.

Everything went all right at the start of the return journey, and the car was doing 175 m.p.h. when a sudden bump jerked me upward in the cockpit. My head was caught by the air-stream, and my goggles were torn away; there was a furious rush of water and sand, which, of course, stung my eyes so that I was temporarily blinded. I had to take a hand from the wheel to clear them, but I managed to keep my foot hard down on the throttle pedal, and by the greatest of good luck the machine remained straight, although a certain amount of speed was lost.

I felt convinced that we had taken the record, and a minute or two after the car stopped it was officially announced that the average speed through the measured mile, for the two runs, was 174·2 m.p.h.; over the kilometre, the speed was 174·8 m.p.h. We had broken the record and *Blue Bird* had gained for itself the title of the fastest car in the world. It was obvious, however, that this new record would not last for long. Segrave's new car was almost complete, while Thomas was ready to make a new attempt at Pendine.

Thomas was ready first. Knowing that Segrave was aiming at 200 m.p.h. with the new Sunbeam, he meant to try and reach this figure himself. It seemed certain that he would break the record which *Blue Bird* held, and that he would exceed 180 m.p.h. at the very least.

On his arrival at Pendine Thomas was recovering from influenza, and his nerves were on edge. Despite his condition he got *Babs* going and made several runs, pausing between each run in order that the carburettor could be readjusted. Then he made another effort—his fifth run of the day—and he was racing towards the measured mile at fully 160 m.p.h. when one of his driving chains broke.

This chain, spinning at tremendous speed, tore through its thin aluminium guard, one end of the chain lashing upward and striking Thomas on the head so that he was killed instantaneously. The car itself pitched into a tremendous skid, leaping off the sand and turning a somersault, landing on its wheels again and sliding to a stop. Helpers rushed to the spot and dragged poor Thomas out, but there was nothing to be done for him. His death marked the first fatal casualty in these efforts to raise the world's land-speed record.

This tragedy was a shock to many men in the motor-racing world. Everybody liked and admired Parry Thomas. He was a wonderful man at his work, always very serious about it, and never in the least conceited about the laurels he gained in races and record-breaking. He was very fond of children, and although he was far from wealthy, it was found after his death that he had maintained a cot in a children's hospital. As a memorial to him his friends and admirers raised a fund to endow the little cot in the hospital for all time—a permanent memorial which Parry Thomas himself would have preferred. As for his wrecked car, a hole was dug in the sands where he died, and the smashed machine was buried there.

IV

FOUR MILES A MINUTE

NOW THAT three-miles-a-minute speed had been almost attained the next step onward in the struggle for the world's land record was 200 m.p.h. and, perhaps before long, four miles a minute.

During the time we were trying to reach 150 m.p.h., there were people who was saying that this mark—if ever it could be attained—would be the limit that cars would ever reach. There were people, again, who, when this figure was passed, refused to believe that anything on wheels would ever touch 200 m.p.h. on land. Subsequent events were to prove them wrong.

When the disaster occurred at Pendine with poor Parry Thomas, Segrave was on his way across the Atlantic with the new Sunbeam, making for Daytona Beach. His car had two twelve-cylinder engines with a total of 44,880 c.c.—more than twice the size of *Blue Bird*, whose record of 174·88 m.p.h. the Sunbeam would now attack.

The Sunbeam turned the scale at four tons and it was about twenty feet in length. It was easily the biggest motor-car that had yet been built, and it was one of the first to be fitted with two engines. Because of its total horse-power it was generally known as the "Thousand-horse-power Sunbeam".

The designers had been very careful about the streamlining, and the car had quite a different appearance from anything which had been previously built. The bodywork was extended to cover the wheels. This made the machine look very broad, and its slug-like appearance and deep red colour helped to make the great machine very striking and formidable.

After Thomas's disaster special investigation was made regarding the safety of the Sunbeam's driving chains. Satisfied on this score, Segrave set out to make his attempt on the world's speed record.

Daytona had been chosen for this attempt as the Pendine Sands—six miles long—did not provide sufficient length. The sands there were also more reliable. This track had already gained fame in America because of record attempts which had been made there. One driver had actually done 180 m.p.h. before Segrave went over, but he had covered the distance in only one direction, so that it did not count for the record.

The course there was marked out over a length of nine miles. This allowed the Sunbeam about four miles in which to get up speed, then came the measured mile, with the remaining four miles in which to slow down.

The Americans were greatly interested about this new attempt. Thousands of people turned out to watch Segrave's trial runs, while the American Automobile Association organized everything on a lavish scale. When the course was cleared for the tests the Sunbeam and its driver faced a stretch of beach nine miles in length, marked by flags and with not a living thing on it, although thousands of spectators had gathered along the adjacent dunes.

Segrave almost met with disaster at the end of his first trial, because his brakes did not work satisfactorily, and he was faced with the alternatives of either charging straight on into the water at the end of the beach or trying to slow the car by turning it towards the sea. He chose the latter, running into shallow water, which pulled the machine up safely without damage.

March 29, 1927, was the day of the actual attempt on the record. It was a day on which Segrave and the 1,000-h.p. Sunbeam made history. The land-speed record was raised to 203·7 m.p.h., and during his fastest run the car reached just 207 m.p.h. Segrave found that colossal wind pressure was his outstanding impression during the effort; it was unimaginably great, and almost lifted his tightly strapped helmet from his head, while his goggles had to be wedged into place. He found, also, that the steering seemed to lag, so that the car did not respond to the wheel until quite an appreciable time had elapsed.

As an indication of how cleverly the capabilities of the machine had been calculated, it may be said that the designers regarded the car as capable of a maximum speed of 215 m.p.h. It might have reached a higher rate of travel had not a different gear ratio been fitted just before the record attempt. This reduced the potential maximum speed to 210 m.p.h.—and the car did 207 m.p.h. Considering that this pace was far greater than anything done before, one need not emphasize that the way in which actual achievement matched theoretical calculations was remarkable.

This speed of 200 m.p.h. marked a definite point in the story of land speed. In the eight years from 1898 to 1906 the record was sent up from 40 m.p.h. to just over 120 m.p.h. It took another nineteen years to raise it by another 30 m.p.h. and to reach 150 m.p.h. The First World War had, of course, intervened and stopped serious attempts on records; yet it was the war itself which made possible the great leap from 150 m.p.h. to over 200 m.p.h.—in just under two years.

During the war research was intensified, the utmost attention being paid to aero engines. The same thing exactly has taken place during the Second World War. In both wars great power has been required for as little weight as possible, making such engines ideal for high-speed cars. It is quite easy to understand that such an engine can be arranged so that it will turn a propeller for an aeroplane as readily as the driving chains or the propeller shaft of a car; it is largely a matter of gearing. The power-units of *Babs* and *Blue Bird* were aero engines, and aero engines were used in the giant record-breakers which, after Segrave had shown the way, were to follow in the efforts to raise the record to speeds which men had hitherto regarded as almost beyond the bounds of possibility.

. . . . .

Segrave's success delighted me; at the same time I realized that despite all the time, trouble and money that had been spent on building *Blue Bird*, the car was now practically useless. It had been designed for a speed of only one hundred and eighty miles an hour, and now here was the big Sunbeam putting that speed twenty-three miles higher. It meant beginning all over again. This after three years of hard work.

The new *Blue Bird*, which in due course came into being, was engined by a Napier-Lion Schneider Trophy aero engine. This engine had twelve cylinders, arranged in three banks of four each, and it gave off about 940 h.p. It was still on the Air Ministry's secret list, but I asked the authorities for permission to install one of these engines in the new car. This request was granted, but a promise had to be given that mechanical details would not be divulged, and that no one would be permitted to examine the unit.

It took the whole of the summer and most of the autumn of 1927 to redesign the car and put in the engine. Extensive wind-funnel tests were carried out at Vickers' works with a new kind of body. These tests showed that exposed wheels created about sixty per cent of the total wind resistance; without the wheels the body formed almost a perfect streamlined shape, in accordance with our knowledge at the time. The resistance provided by the wheels was greatly reduced by building streamlined fairings before and behind them; it was the first time that this had ever been done, reducing the drag from sixty per cent to forty-seven per cent.

Another innovation was a tail-fin, fitted to help stabilize the car while it was travelling at high speed. Two of these fins were made, for use in accordance with whatever wind might be blowing when the car ran, one fin being smaller than the other. In order to remove the resistance offered by a radiator at the front of a car, we fitted two radiators, one either side of the tail and placed end on. This arrangement involved running pipes from the radiators to the front of the engine, two being brought under the driving seat, and two more set one at each side. These pipes promised to become uncomfortably warm when the car was in use, so they were insulated as a protection.

The radiators were not altogether successful in practice, because we found that they travelled in a partial vacuum, and although they did all that was necessary during the record attempt which came later, they were afterwards scrapped. As a sidelight upon the expense attached to the building of such a car, it might be mentioned that these radiators, constructed by a well-known aircraft factory, cost nearly £400 and were eventually sold as scrap metal for five pounds.

An unusual arrangement was in the location of the gear-box, although this had been similar in the old *Blue Bird.* It was placed in front of the driving seat, so that I should have to straddle it, with the clutch pedal on the left, the brake and throttle pedals being on my right, while the gear lever came up between my legs. The gear-box, torque tube and rear-axle casing, formed one solid unit, so that when the car was in action, the big gear-box would be constantly in motion—"floating", as it were—in response to the movement of the back axle.

In this new car quite an amount of material was used which existed in the first *Blue Bird.* The clutch was remodelled, and the gear-box rebuilt, while we employed the same duplicated steering gear, so that each front wheel was directly controlled. The Rudge-Whitworth firm built a set of wheels specially constructed to withstand the great stresses and impacts which would be occasioned by bumps when the car was moving at speed, while their wheels were balanced with the utmost exactitude.

The Dunlop Rubber Company provided the tyres, as they had done both for Segrave and for my own earlier efforts. These tyres were made with the greatest care and thoroughness; each

[Photo: *Keystone Press Agency Ltd.*

Sir Malcolm Campbell's record-breaking *Blue Bird* at speed at Salt Lake City.

[Photo: *St. John Nixon*

S. F. Edge, the famous motorist, in his racing-car. Mr. Edge personally inspects the adjustment and preparation of his car.

[Photo: *Fox Photos Ltd*

Major Segrave's Sunbeam, which reached the record speed of 203.79 m.p.h. in 1927.

[Photo: *Central Press Agency Ltd.*

The Silver Bullet Sunbeam car, designed specially for Mr. Kaye Don's attempt on the speed record.

had a life of about three minutes at 200 m.p.h., and I was advised to change them at the end of each run down the beach. They had no treads at all, because these would have been thrown off at speed; the cord foundation was covered with rubber hardly more than one millimetre in thickness.

All these preparations were, of course, spread over many months, and our hopes were raised when Britain won the Schneider Cup at a speed of 281·49 m.p.h. Our own engine was a duplicate of the one used in the seaplane, and the air contest at Venice told us that we should have all the power we were likely to need. This was encouraging, because rumours were reaching us from the United States concerning cars which were being built there for an attempt on the record. We knew nothing definite, except that the opposition would probably be very strong.

As 1927 drew to a close it grew certain that the spring of the next year would see a very dramatic fight for the land-speed record, because I had now obtained definite information concerning the opposition we should have to face at Daytona, where I had decided to make our effort. At one time there had been indications that at least four American machines would compete, but only two of these actually materialized.

One of these cars had no less than three Liberty aero engines, giving the machine 1,500 h.p.; one of its engines was set in front of the driver, and the other two were placed side by side behind the cockpit. The engines had a total capacity of almost twice that of the 1,000-h.p. Sunbeam which held the record, and nearly four times that of the Napier-Lion engine we were putting into *Blue Bird.*

This American car became known as *Triplex*, and without question it was a leviathan. If power were the only requirement, it appeared as if it must easily beat 203 m.p.h. I heard that 250 m.p.h. was expected, but I knew that so much power would demand very careful work in the designing of the car itself, and that the driver might find it impossible to use all the power at his disposal. All the same, it was certain that the machine would be well-handled, because the chosen driver was Ray Keech, a very experienced man.

The second car which America produced was an altogether different proposition. It was called the *Black Hawk* Stutz, and its design had been supervised by young Frank Lockhart, who was to drive the machine; Lockhart was then about twenty-four years of age. In his twentieth year he had been competing on the California coast in dirt-track events; from this he had gone to board-track work, and afterwards he had raced at Indianapolis. He had also set up wonderful class records on a dry lake-bed, accomplishing most of his work on machines which he himself had tuned.

His car was then the smallest and costliest racing motor-car ever built. It had cost between £20,000 and £30,000, was only three feet in height, two feet in width and fifteen and a half feet in length. It weighed 2,900 pounds, and was shaped like a bullet to lessen wind resistance. It developed about 400 h.p., and the engine turned at 8,000 revolutions per minute when the car was travelling at about 200 m.p.h., while the supercharger ran at 35,000 revolutions a minute.

We left England in February 1928. Our party consisted of four mechanics and myself. We took with us three cases of spare parts, and two special gas engines for starting up the power-unit. There was a big case containing a spare engine, and ten others held spare wheels and tyres. Two more cases were filled with spare parts for the engine and the gear-box. This made eighteen cases in all, apart from the huge crate which contained the car itself.

At Daytona I found my two rivals awaiting me. The fact that three cars were on the scene, each there to launch an individual attack on the record, brought vast crowds, and as it was evident that the efforts would resolve into an international battle, some element of drama was introduced. *Blue Bird* was an invader, but everyone at Daytona did all that was possible to assist us, and we were the first to turn out for preliminary tests.

These tests are always an anxious experience. This one brought us additional worry. *Blue Bird* had never run under her own power, and when we turned out on the beach, with thousands of people watching, I had no idea of how the car would behave, or whether all our calculations would prove correct. My first run almost brought disaster. The sands were not in particularly good condition, and we hit some bumps even before the car began to move at any real speed. Then, with the machine travelling at about 180 m.p.h., we hit a ridge in the sand, and *Blue Bird* leaped clean into the air. For something like thirty feet the car flew forward with all four wheels off the beach, then came down with a jolting thud which jerked me out of my seat. When the car landed the crash shook every bone in my body. A skid followed, but I straightened out and slowed down, bringing the machine to a stop.

When *Blue Bird* was taken back to the garage, we found that part of the under-shield had been torn away, while another section was doubled right up beneath the car. The springs had been damaged, and the shock-absorbers broken. Days of hard work were put in and then, on February 19, I was able to get out on the track again.

The car got away well on its first run, and at about 150 m.p.h. I changed into top gear, then put my foot down hard. With the increasing speed *Blue Bird* altered from a mass of mechanism to something which seemed to be imbued with life and terribly strong. I had actually to wrestle with the car to maintain a straight course, fighting against a tendency to shake from side to side, clinging to the steering-wheel with all my strength. I had time, as we neared the banner which marked the start of the measured mile, to glance at my revolution-counter, which showed that we were doing about 215 m.p.h. After that I kept my gaze ahead.

I could hear the wind screaming past, and my eyes were focused on a point fully a mile in front. The beach rushed to meet me, while all other objects beside the cleared course merged to a blurred and shapeless haze that slashed constantly by. The car accelerated all through the mile, and near the end I dared another glance at the revolution-counter, and this was showing 220 m.p.h. A moment later, and when I had cleared the measured mile, the machine hit a bump. The impact shot me upwards out of my seat and into the truly tremendous air-stream which rushed past the cockpit.

The air felt solid. It tore my goggles from my eyes and forced them down on my face. I was exposed only for the fraction of a second, but the drag felt as if it would jerk me out of the car; I think it would have done but for my grip of the steering-wheel.

If ever I imagined that my end had come, I believed it in the moments which followed, and it was instinctive action which saved my life. I was half-blinded—because of the position of my goggles—and in a machine skidding at over 200 m.p.h. Before I could do anything the car was off the hard surface and in soft sand. Luckily I was able gradually to work the machine out of this, and at the end of another mile was back on the course again, adjusting my goggles and looking for the mechanics who were waiting for me at the far end of the beach. When I stopped I felt exhausted. The muscles of my arms were wrenched and my whole body strained. According to programme, I should have halted to change wheels as a safety measure, but I decided not to do this. I knew that if I stopped and got out of the car, I should never step into the machine again that day. Near the waiting mechanics, I began to turn, then waved to them and started straight back again.

The wind had been behind me on the first run, but it was now against me. I knew that this tended to make the machine even less tractable than it had been before. I had to fight for every yard as we gathered speed for the dash through the measured mile. Just near its entrance I remembered the bump and the soft sand that lay near. If I hit the bump again, and if there was another skid, I knew that I should not have enough strength to hold *Blue Bird*, while the skid would send the car towards the sand dunes, the spectators, and the machines which were parked in front of them.

I held my breath. By good luck, however, we missed it. There was an instant of suspense, then the machine was over the tape, clear of the bump, and racing on with everything flashing past me. I now seemed detached, no part of the blurred world that came to meet the car and vanished behind. I could hear only the rush of the wind, and saw nothing clearly except the far end of the mile.

There were long-drawn-out moments of suspense before I reached it and cleared the tape, then I began to ease my foot on the throttle pedal, doing this very carefully, while the car travelled more than another two miles before I attempted to use the brakes. *Blue Bird* slowed, ran to the end of the course, and stopped. I remained in the cockpit while the mechanics hurried over. I was completely done in, and had to be helped out. Then news came which was like a tonic.

On the first run, *Blue Bird* had covered the measured mile at 214·79 m.p.h., and the return had been at a fraction below 200 m.p.h. The mean speed for the two runs was 206·956 m.p.h., which meant that we had broken the world's land-speed record by a clear margin. Leaning against the side of the car, finding it hard to stand, I realized that we had accomplished all that we had hoped.

. . . . .

The following day, Lockhart and Ray Keech both made trial runs, but without any results as far as breaking the record was concerned. The next day Lockhart brought out his *Black Hawk*. The machine was certainly a picture. It was long and narrow, most marvellously streamlined, and with the wheels hidden by specially fashioned fairings. The car was painted white, and it looked small when compared with *Blue Bird* and *Triplex*. Its appearance may be conveyed by saying that it looked more nearly like a scientific instrument than any car ever before constructed for the record, and, realizing all the work and cleverness behind the machine, one could only wish Frank Lockhart the very best of good fortune.

A misty rain was falling when Lockhart made his start. While the car was travelling at 190 m.p.h. a gust of wind caught it, and before he could regain control his machine dashed into the sea. A huge fountain of water was thrown a hundred feet high; the car, almost too swift to see, leapt high above the waves, crashed in an upflung crowd of spray and leaped again twenty feet above the water. It turned a complete somersault, or in other words looped the loop, and then thundered into the surf, almost buried from sight.

The crowd held its breath. Men rushed across the beach. They plunged into the waves, and reached the car. They were up to their waists, when the high waves broke on them. Suddenly, miraculously, came the cry, "He's alive!"

Lockhart was jammed in the cockpit, imprisoned by the steering-wheel. They tried to drag the car out of the water, but it would not move. At last

200 men and women, linked hand to hand, formed a living chain and by main strength dragged the car out of the water on to the beach.

Wonderful to relate, Lockhart was only partly stunned. His nose was cut and broken, and one of the tendons in his left wrist was severed. The Stutz was badly knocked about, but it was not beyond repair. Next morning he was sitting up in bed planning alterations to his car and fresh speed attempts.

Equally bad luck dogged Ray Keech, who was driving the huge thirty-six-cylinder *Triplex* in a trial run. It was indeed the first run this giant, fantastic motor-car had ever made anywhere.

Nothing like that car had ever been built before, or ever will be again. It was indeed ungainly. The front springs had come off a lorry. The three heavy cross members of the chassis had been taken from a lorry. The three big twelve-cylinder Liberty motors, developing more than 1,500 h.p. in all, had come from an aeroplane.

The Americans estimated that this mechanical giant would accomplish 255 m.p.h. at 2,300 revolutions per minute, allowing 1,000 revolutions to overcome wind resistance and friction.

After some preliminary trials this tremendous machine got under way, and came roaring down the beach at very high speed, only for a water connection to break, so that a scalding shower was blown back on the driver. He retained control of the car and ran to a stop; then he too was rushed off for medical attention.

This accident brought the immediate attempts to an end, but the new record which *Blue Bird* had set up was not allowed to stand for very long. Two months later, Ray Keech reappeared with *Triplex* at Daytona. On April 22, 1928, after a series of runs which were not without danger he succeeded in registering 207·5 m.p.h., just beating what we had done. It was a splendid effort, because he found the car very difficult to hold, while, during his last run, the exhaust pipe badly burnt his right forearm.

The following day, having now completely recovered, Frank Lockhart took his *Black Hawk* out to attack the new record, the car having been completely rebuilt. He worked up the car's speed on two trial runs, then made a third dash southward registering 203·45 m.p.h. After this third run, he turned to come north, and he was approaching the centre of the course at a speed well above 200 m.p.h. when he burst his off-side rear tyre. The car skidded for nearly 500 feet, then made a gigantic leap through the air, jumping for 140 feet and landing on the timing tape. The machine then made a second wild leap of 120 feet, and jumped a third time, covering seventy-five feet before it thudded down on its side. Lockhart was flung out of the car, which came to rest close beside him.

There was no hope for him after such a crash. It brought to an end a career that had hardly begun.

The outcome of these attempts in early 1928 was that the United States held the record. We had decided to try later with *Blue Bird* after a few alterations had been made to the car, when it became known that Segrave was also out to attack the record, using an altogether new and special car which was given the name of *Golden Arrow*.

This remarkable car cost something like £18,000 to build. It had a 930-h.p. Napier-Lion engine, and the machine had a total length of thirty feet, although no point was higher than three feet nine inches from the ground. It was gilded, gaining its name partly from this and partly from the fact that the shape of the engine-cover gave the frontal view the appearance of an arrow-head. A radiator was carried at each side of the machine, and was employed to form a fairing linking the front and rear wheels.

It was calculated that the car's absolute maximum speed would be 246 m.p.h., although it could not actually achieve this owing to loss of speed through wheel-slip. However, it was likely to prove more than fast enough to regain the record for Britain, and in March 1929 Segrave set up wonderful new figures at Daytona. The arrangements for the attempt were more elaborate than any employed before, and in order to indicate either end of the measured mile a powerful red lamp was hung high above the course. When Segrave sighted this, as his car gathered speed, he literally aimed his machine at it, making use of a kind of foresight placed at the front of the car where normally the radiator cap would be found. Visibility was bad during his run, and it was not possible to see more than three-quarters of a mile ahead. He was not troubled by wind pressure, because his screen was specially designed to overcome this, while his cockpit was cut off from the front of the car by a bulkhead, the control pedal working through special leather glands. All these details were largely the result of experience which he had gained during his effort with the 1,000-h.p. Sunbeam.

Segrave's new record was set up with a speed of 231·3 m.p.h.—little less than 24 m.p.h. faster than the old figure—and his success was immediately challenged by *Triplex*. This time the car was in the hands of a new driver named Lee Bible. Unfortunately he was the victim of a grave error of judgment. Either he used his brakes while the car was travelling at too high a speed or, more likely, he released his throttle too abruptly, so that the great engines exercised a braking effect, which sent the car off the course. The tail lifted, then the car swerved and dashed wildly over the soft sand, charging at the dunes beyond, rolling over and over, and becoming a complete wreck.

At the time these events were taking place we had *Blue Bird* over in South Africa. On the strength of highly optimistic reports I had decided to make an attempt on the record at Verneuk Pan. This remote spot lies about 400 miles north of Cape Town. My main reason for going there was a belief that the days of beach records were over, and that for really high speeds something more permanent and less variable than a beach would have to be found. I had already had one miraculous escape from death when the car had skidded into the soft sands at Daytona.

In a later chapter I describe my search for a more suitable track. It was this search which led me to

Verneuk Pan. It was a formidable task transporting the car to this out-of-the-way spot, and on arrival I found I had to face the handicap of driving at an altitude of 3,000 feet above sea-level. Owing to the rarefied atmosphere such a height is bad for carburation and this affects the speed, although this is, to a certain extent, balanced by the lessened air resistance which helps to counter this loss.

As an indication of the organization required in an attempt of this kind I might state that we took with us to South Africa fifty-six cases of spare parts, including R.A.C. timing gear, thirty-six tyres, eight hundred gallons of special fuel, five hundred sparking plugs, and my aeroplane.

The Pan had certain defects which were evident from the start. Not only was it eighty miles from the nearest rail-head and fifty miles from Brandvlei, which formed the nearest link with civilization, but the track itself required a great deal of improving. There were deposits of black pebbles on the lake-bed and, in some places, outcrops of shale with sharp pinnacles sticking up in the hard-baked mud. There were a number of thin bushes growing in patches which also had to be removed. The trouble was labour. There were few natives in this deserted spot, and when a number were sent up from Cape Town, local conditions did not suit them, and many fell sick, while scores deserted.

On my arrival at Verneuk I saw a great, flat space with cliffs dimly visible at the far side. The lake-bed was formed by sun-baked mud, the surface was so smooth that even at high speed there was little perceptible movement of the car. An examination of the surface, however, revealed an unpleasant discovery. Embedded in the mud were little particles of shale; they were sharp-edged and small, and were enough to tear *Blue Bird's* tyres to pieces at speed. I examined other sections of the lake-bed, but everywhere the fragments of shale persisted, and I realized that the car could not be run over such a surface. It looked as though the whole venture would be a failure.

The Provincial Roads Department, however, came to my rescue. It was decided to cover the central fifty feet of a long track with a mixture of mud and water, taking the mud from the lake-bed itself. In other words, the surface was scraped free of shale and an entirely new surface laid down over the whole length of twelve miles. This was an enormous task, for even the water had to be brought from a source five miles away. The smooth surface, flat and free from all pebbles, shale outcrops or fragments of razor-edged stone,

[Photo: *The Topical Press Agency Ltd.*

Motor Racing at Brooklands, April 1928. Malcolm Campbell in his *Blue Bird* car

[Photo: *The Topical Press Agency Ltd.*

The *Blue Bird*, driven by Sir Malcolm Campbell at speed on the track at Brooklands, April 1933.

was almost completed when something occurred which was the equivalent to a local miracle.

A shower of rain fell on the Pan, to be followed by a torrential downpour, the first for twenty years. The storm did much damage to our camp, cars and lorries bogged, and when dawn broke, the lake-bed lay under six inches of water. We were cut off from the world for a week, and, towards the end, we lived on tinned salmon, brackish water and native bread which had a peculiar aniseed taste.

Just prior to the coming of the rains I encountered another misfortune. One day I went up in a light aeroplane piloted by a South African with the intention of surveying the track from the air. The machine had only climbed sixty feet when she stalled and crashed. She was completely wrecked, my nose was almost entirely torn off, my lips were cut, and I was banged on the head on exactly the same place where, a year before, the bonnet of a car had flown off while I was driving at 100 m.p.h. at Brooklands, and almost fractured my skull.

I managed to stumble out of the machine and wired to Cape Town for my own Moth to be sent up to Verneuk. Major Allister Miller, South Africa's famous pilot, flew the machine up in the course of a few hours. On his arrival I at once arranged to fly back with him to Cape Town, although my head and face were swathed in bandages. Miller landed the Moth perfectly in a gale of wind, but a sudden gust of wind tilted it sideways. It turned over—and re-opened all my wounds.

My third and final misfortune occurred just after the course had started to dry up after the floods. I had flown to Cape Town to celebrate my birthday; in the evening something arrived, however, which, as a birthday gift, I could only receive with mixed feelings. It took the form of a message advising me that, during the afternoon, Segrave had broken the world's record. He had raised it from 207 m.p.h. to 231·36 m.p.h.

What this meant may be appreciated from the fact that with the engine turning over at maximum revolutions, *Blue Bird* was capable of a theoretical speed of 231·8 m.p.h.—making no allowance for wheel-slip or for the loss of power occasioned by the high altitude.

Blue Bird could not possibly beat Segrave's speed. We were defeated, and after being on the course for six weeks, we had not yet had a chance to run our car.

We had gone so far, so much time and money had been spent, that there could be no question of returning to England without giving *Blue Bird* a chance to show what she could do. I still wanted to try for the land-speed record, although I was sure that we could not break the new figure; in any case, we could attempt world's long-distance records and perhaps set up new speeds over five miles. Success in this might offer some recompense to those who had worked, and were still working, on the course.

We continued almost as if nothing had happened, and help came from every hand. We were all imbued by a hope that, somehow, *Blue Bird* might yet beat 231 m.p.h.; I knew that this was a technical impossibility, yet we intended to try.

The work of construction continued. The job of bringing *Blue Bird*, packed in a case, over the 400 miles' journey to the Pan, brought its full share of difficulties, which were, however, overcome. I arranged to drive for records on April 20, having in the meantime been discharged from hospital.

Owing to the presence of mirages on the Pan, it was necessary to make our tests as soon after daylight as possible. We breakfasted hastily, then the machine was pushed down to the starting point; a crowd of spectators had gathered, having apparently come from nowhere during the night. The engine was warmed up and I slipped into the cockpit, while the car was pushed forward until it straddled the white line. Very soon after that, I sent *Blue Bird* away on her first run.

I did not start with the intention of doing more than test the car, but the machine accelerated in the most amazing way on that even surface, and the revolution-counter had shown 215 m.p.h. before I pulled up at the far end of the line. I discovered one or two bumps, and was troubled by engine fumes, but the test was most satisfactory. Our enthusiasm rose once again, because the trial gave prospects of a good finish to all our efforts.

We had planned to run next day with the car officially timed, but a wind sprang up over the Pan and it seemed better to wait until this died down. It vanished that night, but returned more strongly than ever after dawn on the next day, a Sunday, when we were warned that there were indications of more rain within the next few days. When the wind ceased, early on Sunday afternoon, we decided to make our attempt on Segrave's record, and the car was rolled from the marquee to the starting point.

It was my intention to open right out. I did not think I could beat the *Golden Arrow's* speed, but nothing could be lost by trying to do so. The machine was made ready, I settled down in the cockpit, and soon *Blue Bird* was accelerating down the broad white line which had been painted on the surface to indicate direction, gathering speed just as splendidly as she had done before.

The line slid under the nose of the machine and was swallowed up, and I found it a splendid guide as the car ran towards the start of the measured mile. I had the throttle full open then, and it was not easy to hold the car. Once I had crossed the timing tape, the bumps seemed worse, but the machine behaved very well. I glanced at the revolution-counter while I was in the measured distance, and saw it showing rather more than 230 m.p.h.

My hopes were high when I reached the end of the course and turned. A great cloud of dust had been raised by the car, and this hung above the track, drifting slowly away on the wind. I wondered what speed had been registered, and there seemed a chance that I might yet break the record—although only by a very narrow margin—if the return run was as fast as the first one. I restarted, and my experience was much the same as on the outward journey, except that I could feel that the machine was not so fast. The mud service was friable, and had been cut up by the earlier runs, and this slowed the car. When I stopped, I found that the recorded speed on the first trip had been 225·5 m.p.h., and on the return run *Blue Bird* had reached 212·5 m.p.h., giving an average speed of 219 m.p.h. for the mile—a long way below Segrave's figure.

I had expected that, and it had been too much to hope for more. The car had run wonderfully, and now we made arrangements to try for the five-miles' record—which stood at 140·6 m.p.h.—and for the five kilometres; Segrave had taken the latter during his run at Daytona with 202·7 m.p.h. I felt sure that *Blue Bird* could pass both speeds, although I had been warned by Dunlops that my tyres were intended only for the mile, and had not been built for a sustained effort over five times that distance. I decided to risk this.

The timing tapes were so arranged that I had about three miles in which to get up speed before the car entered the measured five miles, then came another three miles in which to slow down and stop from over 200 m.p.h.

During the next few days the wind became stronger, and dust-storms swept the Pan. We found that the wind died at night, and did not come up again until about half an hour after dawn. We judged that, if we had the car ready, the attempts on the five-miles' record could be made in the still air immediately after dawn. This would have to be done before sunrise, because the track was set from east to west; if the car ran after the sun came up, I should be driving straight into its rays.

We brought the car out an hour before dawn. The course was examined and found to be clear, the engine was warmed up and switched off, then I waited in the cockpit until there should be sufficient light by which to drive.

The time passed slowly. When I could see well, I asked the mechanics to start up the engine. It sulked, but finally they got it going and the men gathered at the tail to push the car away and relieve the load on the clutch. I sent the machine off, but it stopped after a hundred yards or so. They raced after it and restarted the engine; this time, *Blue Bird* went away excellently, roaring down the white line.

I used all *Blue Bird's* power of acceleration, but the machine was still short of maximum speed when I crossed the first timing tape. The car gathered pace as it roared on, covering the whole five miles at well above 210 m.p.h. I slowed without difficulty, and turned round, then stopped close to the mechanics who waited there. They looked the car over and changed the wheels, the tyres being so badly cut that no tread remained. Then I started back.

The wheels spun as *Blue Bird* got away, and this stripped the thin rubber tread from the near-side rear tyre. For the whole of the return journey, the car was running on the canvas of that tyre, and the fact that it did not burst is a tribute to the men who made it.

The average speed over five kilometres proved to be 216·03 m.p.h.—beating Segrave's record for this distance—and the pace over the five miles was 211 m.p.h., 70 m.p.h. faster than the existing record.

With this success we had to be content; we had used all the tyres we had brought out, and no more were available. We packed up and began the journey home. My last memory of Verneuk Pan is of the long white line gleaming in the sunshine, and the cleared space of the course stretching like a scar across the lake-bed. This—and *Blue Bird* rolling slowly across on a big lorry.

That deserted and desolate scene helped to bring home the fact that the car had reached the highest speed of which it was capable. It could have no hope of beating the new record of 231 m.p.h. Once again we were faced with a situation which had arisen before; we had a machine which had been outclassed, just as the original *Blue Bird* had been two years before. We had started for Verneuk Pan with the hope of beating 207·5 m.p.h.; this we had done, but, in the meantime, the record had been raised still higher. Once more I had to decide whether I would abandon these record attempts, or whether we should build a new car and try again.

. . . . .

Just about this time a new competitor entered the field for world's record honours. This was a new Sunbeam of 4,000 h.p., which was to be driven by Kaye Don. The car eventually became known as the *Silver Bullet*, and it had two twelve-cylinder engines, each of 2,000 h.p., set one behind the other, making the car one enormous mass of machinery.

Work had been going forward on this car for almost a year, but its details were not revealed until the end of 1929, and even then it was a couple of months before the machine was actually seen by anyone other than those who were working on it. It proved to be thirty-one feet in length, with a blank, rounded nose, twin stabilizing fins at the tail, and fairings between the wheels. When Kaye Don was in the cockpit, he had about twenty feet of bonnet in front of him.

The *Silver Bullet* must have been the highest-powered car ever built, because it had more horse-power even than *Triplex*, great as this American machine had been. Kaye Don took the car to Daytona in March 1930 and remained there for some weeks. Adverse conditions delayed his attempts on the record, and when he did get the car going he was unable to register more than about 180 m.p.h. He abandoned his efforts and the *Silver Bullet* came home to stand derelict and idle.

While Kaye Don was at Daytona, plans for a new *Blue Bird* were completed. We had decided to build a new car, but to use as much of the old one as possible, although it was evident that not a great deal of the original machine could be employed. The work of reconstruction was put in hand and continued all through 1930. We fitted a new supercharged Napier-Lion engine giving 1,450 h.p., while construction was so arranged that I should be able to sit beside the propeller shaft, and thus secure a much lower position in the cock-pit, thus reducing wind resistance. We estimated that the machine should be able to reach about 240 m.p.h., and one of our greatest problems was to keep the rear driving wheels on the ground, so that they would not jump and spin uselessly in the air, thus dissipating power.

This problem of what is known as "wheel adhesion" is of first importance. It is easy to understand that unless the wheels are kept on the ground much speed is lost. For this reason we did not attempt to make *Blue Bird* light in weight. Up to a point, the heavier the car the greater the chance of success, as will be appreciated from the fact that we actually carried between twelve to fourteen hundredweight of lead ballast.

The total length of the car was some twenty-five feet, and its very size presented certain difficulties, particularly with the wheels. Each of these, when complete with tyres, weighed two hundredweight, and three men were needed to change one wheel, an operation which took some time. We foresaw that it might not be possible to change wheels between runs at Daytona where, according to the regulations, a second run must be made within half an hour of the completion of the first, if the registered speeds are to count for the record. In view of this, and because it was doubtful if a wheel-change could be effected in the half-hour allowed, I decided to make each set of tyres do for the double run on the course.

Blue Bird, accompanied by no less than twenty cases containing spare parts, tools, and equipment, crossed the Atlantic for Daytona in January

1931. We experienced a great deal of trouble during this effort. Throughout the first trials visibility was so bad on the beach that I actually lost all touch with my position while I was travelling at speed. There are no landmarks beside the course, and I was moving at about 180 m.p.h. when I suddenly discovered myself near the end of the cleared stretch, dashing at spectators and parked cars lined up behind the place where my mechanics waited. Fortunately I was able to pull up in time, but only about forty yards short of the crowd, and after some quite desperate gear changing and braking.

On another run my revolution-counter was showing a speed of 260 m.p.h. when the gear lever jumped out of mesh, and it was only by good fortune that the engine did not blow up altogether, because its revolutions raced to the absolute limit. During the actual attempt the car swung off the course, and I was faced with the choice of slowing down and trusting that I should be able to bring the car back into position. I kept my foot down, and the car answered willingly, although it got into a bad swing. I was able to hold it, however.

On completing the two runs, my mechanics rushed to meet me and I learned that the speed for my first run had been 246·575 m.p.h., and that the return had been made at 244·897 m.p.h., giving a speed for the record of 245·736 m.p.h.

We had raised the record by over 14 m.p.h. from Segrave's old figure of 231·3 m.p.h., and *Blue Bird* secured the honour of being the first land-speed machine ever to achieve a speed of four miles a minute.

The car might have been faster, but for the wet sand on the beach, which had formed a drag on the wheels, and it would certainly have set the record higher but for the earlier mishap with the gear lever which had robbed the engine of its best tune.

V

FIVE MILES A MINUTE

AFTER the record run which I have just described, a paper appeared with a comment under *Senseless Speed Records.* "If there are people in this country who wish to travel at the rate of 240 m.p.h., they will hail Captain Campbell as a benefactor of the race. Most of those who have had that sort of itch in the past, however, are to-day resting under headstones. . . . We have seen no predictions from any quarter that a speed of 240 m.p.h. by a motor-driven vehicle will ever be of the slightest use to anybody. . . . In the air, speed is of practical use in shortening distances and saving time. On land super-speed machines like that driven by Captain Campbell are of interest only as providing the swiftest known means of travelling from good health to the graveyard."

Comment of that nature was bound to arise; I had seen similar observations years before, when four miles a minute had appeared quite out of reach. The man who wrote those words had not appreciated certain viewpoints. Breaking the record was an achievement, taken by itself alone; it was the result of an effort as personal as that of an athlete trying to run a mile in shorter time than anyone has ever done. Everyone applauds the runner and, if he is successful, congratulates him upon setting a new mark; any strain, or any physical risk he may run, is his own affair—just as it would have been my own misfortune if anything had gone wrong at 240 m.p.h.

The athlete, however, cannot be said to contribute very largely to the world's work, but breaking the world's land-speed record actually does benefit a large number of people. The country responsible for the car gains in prestige, it proves the ability of its craftsmen in the production of material and workmanship which is unsurpassed. The very great amount of research work necessary to create the machine obliges scientists to make quite detailed investigations in metallurgy, road holding, and streamlining, and to overcome problems of transmission and braking. These problems would not otherwise be set, and the knowledge which their solution brings can be applied to everyday machines; this, in its turn, brings improvements in design and helps to make more stable and roadworthy the cars which are driven on the roads in the ordinary way.

The newspaper was, of course, at liberty to express its point of view, and to call the record attempts "senseless". At the same time, such an outlook seems very restricted—it is much on a par with that ill-chosen political slogan "Safety First" which did us so much harm in the years prior to the Second World War. I doubt, however, if this outlook is general. In fact, the overwhelming congratulations which I received at Daytona, after the run, showed the opinion of America as a whole.

I was fêted to an embarrassing extent, and it was the more difficult to accept these congratulations since I appreciated that the success was not due to myself alone. Behind me were the engineers and scientists, the designers and the workmen who had constructed the car, while I owed more than it is possible to express to the loyal work of Villa and Leech and the rest of my mechanics; it would have been impossible to find a keener and more efficient little group of men.

. . . . .

Blue Bird did not return to Britain directly after the Daytona run. The car was sent to the

British Empire Exhibition at Buenos Aires where it remained for three weeks, providing much interest to the crowds who visited its stand. During this time Norman Smith—nicknamed "Wizard" Smith—in New Zealand was actively preparing for an attack on the new figure of 246 m.p.h. Some time previously he had built a big car and had tried it out. His machine was the subject of many modifications before he seriously attacked the record.

His modified car had some frontal resemblance to the *Golden Arrow*, and was fitted with two stabilizing fins, while its engine was a duplicate of that employed in *Blue Bird*. The machine had been designed to reach 300 m.p.h., and this was so wide a margin above the record that there was a possibility of Smith achieving success, although it hardly seemed likely that he would break the record on his first attempt.

It is easy to understand the fact that we wanted to keep the record in England, but I did not, at this time, intend to make another effort unless the record was broken. It was necessary, however, to be prepared for this eventuality, and it was decided that Railton, who had been responsible for *Blue Bird* in its existing form, should take the car over on its return from South America, and do all that was required to make the machine capable of replying to any speed which Smith might set up at Ninety Mile Beach where he was making his effort.

Fortune did not smile upon Norman Smith. He intended making full use of the beach, taking a run of nearly eight miles in which to get up speed before entering the measured distance. I expected, from day to day, to hear that he had been successful, but his efforts failed.

Work had been going forward during the whole of the summer on *Blue Bird*, and the car was almost ready to attempt to raise the record. Although Smith had been unsuccessful, he intended to try again, and I knew that an American racing driver had got out designs for a car to run at Daytona. It seemed that *Blue Bird's* figures might soon be attacked.

Now, with *Blue Bird* ready, there was no reason why the car should stand idle. Also, there was a new mark at which to aim, although it stood only a little distance beyond the figures I had already set up. Years before, I had reached 146 m.p.h. and had then become ambitious to be the first man to do 150 m.p.h. Now I had achieved 246 m.p.h.—and 250 m.p.h. lay only a little distance away. It seemed worth while trying to reach this speed.

When I was still in a state of indecision, I

received a cable; it came soon after New Year's Day, 1932, and was from the Mayor of Daytona: *The City of Daytona Beach invites you and offers every co-operation to further your attempt to create a new world record.*

This decided me. I accepted the invitation, and thus committed myself to at least one more attempt.

. . . . .

Blue Bird had not been greatly altered in appearance except that the radiator had been given a slightly longer cowling, and wind resistance had been further reduced. Tail-fin, wheel fairings, bodywork and chassis remained the same, but we had changed the engine for the one which we had previously taken to Daytona as a spare. Minor modifications to the power unit were expected to give the car about fifty more horse-power, while the Daytona authorities made every effort to provide the machine with a good chance of showing what it could do. They agreed to a proposal to increase the length of the course by making use of the sands at the north side of the pier.

The existence of this structure limited the distance available in which to get up speed before entering the measured mile. The piles of the pier were set fifty feet apart, and the plan was to start the car some distance north of this and drive under the pier at about 140 m.p.h. *Blue Bird* would thus be travelling at this speed when the car reached the spot from which earlier attempts had been started.

It was early in February 1932 that *Blue Bird*, the mechanics and myself arrived at Daytona. I was immediately informed that beach conditions were not likely to be favourable for some time, and personal inspection showed that they were quite impossible. The weather was ideal, but the wind acting on the waves had had an unusual effect upon the sand. Instead of being flat, it now came down in a curve from high-water mark to the sea. It was not feasible to drive very fast over this cambered beach, while the surface was very uneven.

There was nothing we could do but wait for the wind to change. In the meantime I surveyed the beach carefully, and saw that the extension beyond the pier would enable us to do more than attack the mile record only. At Verneuk Pan, we had set up new figures for the five kilometres and the five miles; by taking advantage of the longer run at Daytona, it would be possible for *Blue Bird* to attack these records. In effect, we could attempt no less than five records during the one effort;

these were the one kilometre, one mile, five kilometres, five miles and ten kilometres. The speed for the last stood at about 152 m.p.h., but all the others were above 210 m.p.h.

It was a week before the wind veered round and conditions became a little better. *Blue Bird* was towed to the beach for a trial test. Conditions, however, were still so bad that I had the worst ride I have ever known from the viewpoint of comfort. Knowing the state of the beach, I had strapped myself in, and but for this I should probably have been jerked out of the car. I felt absolutely fit when I began the run, but I was very bruised and tired when I brought *Blue Bird* back to her starting-point, my best speed through the mile having been recorded as well below 140 m.p.h. Still, apart from the bruising, I knew that there was nothing wrong with the car itself.

There followed some more days of unsatisfactory weather conditions—a state of affairs which is not only trying but makes one impatient. Still, in due course, things did get better and I was able to take *Blue Bird* out on the beach for what was meant to be another test run. I intended, however, to try for the records if it proved possible, although I knew that the beach was not as smooth as it might have been.

I remained waiting in the cockpit for what seemed an age before we received the word to start, then the car was pushed off, and I sent it towards the dark outline of the pier. It rushed to meet me as *Blue Bird* accelerated, then I shot between the piles and the open beach showed ahead. A side wind seemed to increase in force as the speed mounted, while with my foot hard down on the accelerator pedal, I watched for the first timing strip.

Before I picked this up and when the car was doing about 230 m.p.h., the wheels ran into a patch of water, which rose over the front in a shower of spray and smashed against my goggles. I was completely blinded as the car raced on and, for some moments, my heart seemed to stand still because, at such speed, the machine could leave the course in the fraction of time. Then, after a lapse of about two seconds, I was able to see again, and discovered that *Blue Bird* had already begun to swerve towards the sea. I straightened out and sighted the red panel, heading for it with the throttle pedal rammed flat.

Because of the roughness of the beach, it required all my strength to hold the wheel, which was kicking under my hands all the time and this blistered my palms badly. When I was half-way through the mile I glanced at the revolution-counter, which showed 3,800 revolutions per minute, equivalent to a road speed of 273 m.p.h. I knew that the car must actually be travelling more slowly than this owing to wheel-slip.

I cleared the mile and continued flat out until *Blue Bird* was beyond the end of the ten kilometres before I began to slow down. I was able to reduce speed without difficulty, and stopped at the end of the course. I halted only long enough to wipe my goggles and, not waiting to change tyres, began the return run. The wind was now against the machine, and I could feel its effect as the speed rose. Gusts caught the car constantly, and again I was troubled by flying water while I could feel that the machine was appreciably slower. I cleared the timing tapes, picked up the pier again and ran between the piles at about 150 m.p.h; this proved to be quite easy and did not present much difficulty.

Within a very short time, I knew the registered speeds. On the first run, the car had gone through the mile at 267·4 m.p.h., and the run north, against the wind, had been accomplished at 241·7 m.p.h., which gave me a mean speed over the mile of 253·9 m.p.h.—eight miles an hour faster than the old record.

The speed through the kilometre had worked out at 251·3 m.p.h. We had also broken the five kilometres record with 241·5 m.p.h., but, unhappily, the timing equipment controlling the five miles and ten kilometres distances had broken down and the speeds had not been taken.

This was disappointing but, in any case, I felt that *Blue Bird* could go much faster if there were no hampering wind. We decided to try again next day, partly because I wanted to lift the mile record still higher, and also because I wanted to register a new record for five miles and ten kilometres. We could not attack the ten miles record because the beach was too short.

We had everything ready the following day, and the sand was excellent, but it was raining and the Mayor of Daytona refused to allow us to make the attempt. The next day the morning was bright, the wind reduced, but the beach was covered with ripples and was very wet. It looked as if I might be in for a rough ride, and this proved to be the case after *Blue Bird* had started.

I was bumped about a good deal on the approach to the measured mile, but crossed the timing tapes with the car absolutely all out. I saw 4,000 r.p.m. on the revolution-counter, which was equal to 287 m.p.h. but, at times, the uneven sand was kicking the back wheels off the ground, causing wheel-spin and, actually, the car was much slower through the mile than it had been two days before. No new record was set up over this distance, but *Blue Bird* succeeded in creating fresh records for the longer stretches.

The car's pace over five kilometres was now 247·9 m.p.h., more than thirty miles an hour faster than the record made at Verneuk Pan. The five miles were covered at 242·7 m.p.h., also over thirty miles an hour faster. And the speed over the ten kilometres—equivalent to six and a quarter miles—was 238·6 m.p.h., an improvement by some 75 m.p.h. on the existing record.

I would have tried again, because I was convinced that *Blue Bird* could have done better still through the mile, but the attempts had to end on that day. However, we had lifted the land-speed record to 253·9 m.p.h., which was well above the 250 m.p.h. we had hoped to reach, while the car had actually recorded 267 m.p.h. on one run. In all, we had secured five world's records, despite the fact that the car had visited the beach only three times.

. . . . .

In actual time, *Blue Bird's* fastest run in 1932 had involved travelling through the measured mile in only one and one-fifth seconds less than the car's best performance the year before, yet this represented the difference in speed between 246·5 m.p.h. and 267·4 m.p.h. Had the car been one and a half seconds faster still, it would have travelled at 300 m.p.h.

These small differences in times show that in efforts on raising records machine and man must be tuned to a very high pitch of efficiency, if they are to reach beyond the limit that has previously been attained. All the effort which has already been made must be made again, with just a little more effort added.

Even though travelling at 267 m.p.h. occupied only 13·46 seconds, and although 300 m.p.h. means only twelve seconds, the difference between these two times—just 1·46 seconds—demands a great deal. This difference seems very small, and the difficulty in reducing it lies almost wholly in the fact that all that has been achieved must be gone over again. Even at the risk of repetition, it seems as well to stress this, because it lies behind the reasons why I made up my mind to try and lift the record to 300 m.p.h., after the Daytona effort in 1932.

I had been the first man to do three miles a minute, the first to reach four miles a minute, and it promised much in personal achievement if I could be the first to reach five miles a minute on land. I wanted to do it because I felt that once the goal of 300 m.p.h. had been reached, there was a possibility that the record might stand for Britain for some time to come. It would, truly, be a mark of the excellence of British engineering.

I felt, also, that I had been given unique opportunities of making such an attempt. Quite by chance, I had gained more experience of very high speed work than most men, and it seemed advisable to put this to good use, although I had now gone far past the age when a man may expect, normally, to endure the strain which would be entailed. Still I felt capable of meeting the physical and mental stress of future record effort.

It was plain from what I already knew, that 300 m.p.h. could not be achieved in one single effort. The record had been pushed up only in gradual stages. In survey, the figures showed as: 150—152 — 169 — 171 — 174 — 203 — 206 — 207 — 231 — 246 — and, now, 253 m.p.h.

Although I had reached 267 m.p.h. in actual speed, this did not stand for the record; to attain 300 m.p.h., the official figure had to be lifted by almost another 50 m.p.h. That increase had never been made in one effort, and now that the fraction of time necessary had become still more difficult to win, it was obvious that five miles a minute would be fully as difficult to reach as anything which had been done before; I judged that it would require at least two more attempts. If the mark was gained after only one intermediate effort, it would be only by good luck.

Whatever might be involved, I resolved to try, and this decision was in my mind when we reached England, where a marvellous reception awaited us. There were people ready to suggest that enough had been done, but I felt our work was unfinished.

There had been a time when 146 m.p.h. had looked an odd figure, and I wanted to lift the record speed to 150 m.p.h.; now, 253 m.p.h. looked an odd figure, and I wanted to raise it to 300 m.p.h. This speed formed a possible seal on all that had already been done, although I knew that it could be beaten, because five miles a minute does not form a limit of land speed. Given the right surface, a long enough run, and a car designed for the work, a man may reach even 500 m.p.h. The limiting factor to ultimate speed will be the difficulty of finding a suitable course, not in the cars themselves or in the human element. This matter, however, I have gone into more fully in the final chapter of this book.

There had been a time when 180 m.p.h. appeared so far away that it seemed phenomenal. When Segrave took the record for the first time at Daytona, newspaper placards appeared with the simple legend: 203 *m.p.h.* The announcement needed no qualifications; in fact, even newspaper men found it difficult to discover words which would adequately express the amazement aroused by Segrave's feat.

Since then, *Blue Bird* had reached such speeds that 200 m.p.h. was regarded only as a reasonable pace for an initial test run. In view of this, it would be unwise to suggest that any new record could not be beaten, or that land speed would rise to a particular figure and then remain stationary.

So far as *Blue Bird* was concerned, I did not think we could reach out beyond 300 m.p.h., and if we did attain this speed, we should have done well. In the months following our return we began work on the car, with the definite intention of travelling to Daytona for the speed trials in 1933. When the machine reached England, I drove it in an exhibition run at Brooklands—when wheel-spin tore the rear tyres to shreds—then *Blue Bird's* reconstruction was started without delay.

. . . . .

During 1932, "Wizard" Smith had tried again with his car at Ninety Mile Beach, but he had not been successful and, as the year drew near its end, it appeared that he had abandoned his attempts. There was a crop of rumours concerning possible contenders at Daytona, but none of the projected cars had materialized by the time that reconstruction of *Blue Bird's* chassis had been completed, enabling us definitely to plan for another effort which, I hoped, would be a step towards 300 m.p.h.

Reid A. Railton, at Thompson and Taylor's, was responsible for the alteration and modifications which had been carried out, and we had now given the car a new engine. This was a Schneider Trophy-type Rolls-Royce of 2,500 h.p., nearly half as powerful again as the power unit we had last used for the record. Its incorporation had necessitated extensive alterations, and the appearance of the car was much changed.

My acquisition of the Rolls-Royce engine was an essential factor in the building of the new *Blue Bird*. On many previous occasions I had discussed with the Rolls-Royce firm the possibility of obtaining one of their special engines, but each time without success. Now, rather to my surprise and certainly to my delight, my request was granted. They agreed to sell me the engine I wanted. This meant everything to future success.

The radiator was covered by a cowling in which an air-scoop was set to feed the supercharger. Instead of allowing air to rush through the radiator and find its way through an opening behind, the top of the cowling now formed part of the engine-cover, and the air emerged through apertures at the sides.

Our greatest problem was to make use of all the power available and, to accomplish this, it was virtually necessary to maintain wheel adhesion; unless the wheels were kept on the ground, speed would be lost and we could not snatch the seconds we wanted to gain. We could not rely upon the tyres to maintain a grip on the sand, because their treads were quite smooth and were very thin, and we had considered the possibility of building a machine in which all four wheels were driven, but this construction would have been most costly.

The very fact that the new attempt was to reach out a little beyond anything that had been done before, imposed certain restrictions on the car itself; in other words, there were definite limits to the stress that its mechanism could withstand. If, for instance, any attempt was made to run the machine at full speed for more than ninety seconds, the gear-box and the back axle might fail under the strain; this was not likely to occur, because Daytona Beach was not long enough to permit such a high speed to be sustained for a minute and a half.

Theoretically, it was possible to do 100 m.p.h. on first gear, 200 m.p.h. on second gear, and well over 300 m.p.h. in top speed, but we estimated that to reach five miles a minute a run of seven miles would be necessary before entering the measured mile, while an absolutely smooth beach would also be required. Daytona lacked the necessary length, and we could not expect perfect conditions. In fact, before the car was shipped to America, we anticipated setting new figures at somewhere between 270 m.p.h. and 280 m.p.h.; this would be an extremely satisfactory step towards the 300 m.p.h. which might be attained at some later date.

The tyres were again made by Dunlops, after very careful tests, and were tried out on a machine capable of giving the equivalent of 310 m.p.h. The manufacturers considered them to be the finest tyres they had constructed up to that date, and their care is demonstrated by the fact that they used a special Egyptian fibre in the cord; this fibre flexed easily, and helped to keep the tyres cool. A special rubber was used for the treads,

[Photo: *Keystone Press Agency Ltd.*

Sir Malcolm Campbell and his 300 m.p.h. *Blue Bird* in 1933.

[Photo: *Fox Photos Ltd.*

With typical American pageantry at Daytona Beach, Florida, the British competitor and his crew of mechanics are posed for a photograph.

compounded to make it more effective in reducing the rasping effect of the Daytona sand. The tyres were designed to run at a pressure of 125 pounds, but even then they would expand an inch in diameter at speed.

The car was twenty-seven feet long. The increased length lent a more graceful appearance, and did much to help make it the most impressive of all the *Blue Birds* which had so far been built.

. . . . .

The City of Daytona surpassed itself by its welcome when I stepped off the train on February 2, 1933. There was an enormous crowd waiting at the station, headed by police, city officials, and members of the Racing Association, accompanied by a band. This band marched at the head of a procession to the hotel, where I found my room filled with flowers sent by friends that I had made in America.

The long journey from New York had been something of a strain and I was still suffering from the effects of influenza. I did not regret, therefore, a fortnight's delay, due to bad weather and beach conditions, before I was able to take *Blue Bird* out for a test, a band of the American Legion, wearing blue tunics and orange trousers, marching ahead of the machine. The beach was far from good, but I wanted to try out the car.

Right from the start, I was in trouble. The sand was so rough that it was hard to steer a straight course, and real difficulties arose when I tried to change into top gear. This was never easy and, in forcing the lever home, I strained the tendons of my left hand, wrenching muscles and tendons all the way up my forearm.

The surface became worse when I entered the measured mile and here, because of the pain in my left arm, I drove almost one-handed, and this did not make the car easier to handle. Again and again *Blue Bird* edged off the course, once swerving dangerously near to the sea. To make matters worse, fumes came into the cockpit, but I did my best to keep the car travelling at a reasonable speed.

In spite of everything, *Blue Bird* registered 227 m.p.h. over the mile, and averaged about 180 m.p.h. along a five-mile stretch, which accomplished all that I had set out to do, and I learned enough about the car to decide that the gear ratio should be lowered, while the clutch needed some adjustment.

I did not make a return run. My hand was too painful, and I felt a little sick as a result of the fumes; some means of preventing these getting into the cockpit had to be found before I attempted the record. *Blue Bird* was towed back to the garage, where work began at once on the changes required.

It was not until a week later that *Blue Bird* was ready again. Even then, there were shells on the beach and the sand was still rough; I should have made no more than a test run, but for the fact that we had been waiting so long. I arranged that tyres should be changed after the first run, because they were certain to be cut about by the shells. In addition, visibility was not very good.

There was a considerable delay before we received the word to go. The huge crowd watched the engine started. Flames shot from the exhaust, smoke rolled behind, then *Blue Bird* went away to a good start but, as the car gathered speed, it seemed to skate on the wet sand, and I could feel the rear wheels kicking from the bumps long before I changed into top gear.

I had to work hard to keep the machine straight, and I was so shaken and jarred in the cockpit that it was not easy to keep my foot on the accelerator pedal as I sent the car into the measured mile. As I crossed the timing tape I looked at the revolution-counter and, according to the position of the needle, *Blue Bird* was travelling at 328 m.p.h.

I knew that wheel-slip was reducing the actual speed, but I knew that I was travelling very fast indeed, and it felt very dangerous. The pace held until I had cleared the mile, then I began to ease up, watching for the lorry and the mechanics at the far end. When I halted near them, they ran to the machine at once and began the work of changing the wheels, finding the tyres badly cut about by shells, as we had anticipated.

While I stopped, a man massaged my left arm, which felt very strained, and while he was working I was told that my speed during that run had been 273·556 m.p.h. This was much higher than the record we had set up a year earlier, but it was over fifty miles an hour below the speed which my revolution-counter had shown during the run through the mile.

Obviously, the difference was entirely due to wheel-spin. The sand was too rough to permit the use of full throttle; the probability was that the car would be just as fast—and possibly faster—at a lesser throttle opening on the return run.

My left arm was very painful and I felt all in; after a halt of almost twenty minutes, *Blue Bird* began the second run. At once the weakness of my left hand become evident, while, for some reason, the car "snaked" more than before. Again and again the machine swung out of the straight as speed mounted, so I had to fight for control.

One vicious swerve carried me within a yard of the marking flags along the course, just as I came within sight of the measured mile. I pulled the car back, then glanced at my revolution-counter and saw it showing what should have been a road-speed of over 300 m.p.h. I eased my foot, so that the throttle pedal was depressed to only about three-quarters of its full travel; this meant that not so much power was being given to the engine, yet when *Blue Bird* entered the mile, the needle still showed 300 m.p.h.

Somehow, I managed to keep my foot steady, working all the while to maintain a straight course, then, clearing the far end of the mile, I began to slow, realizing that the effort was over and that I could hardly fail to have broken the record. I ran to the depot by the pier and pulled up, to be informed—within a minute or so—that *Blue Bird's* speed over the second run had been 270·676 m.p.h.

This gave me an average of 272·1 m.p.h. We had raised the land-speed record by nearly twenty miles an hour and, incidentally, we had set up a new five-kilometre record with 257·2 m.p.h.—ten miles faster than the speed of the year before.

. . . . .

On the first run I had travelled with the throttle pedal pushed absolutely flat, so that the engine was giving out all the power of which it was capable, but wheel-spin had reduced the car's speed. On the return, I used three-quarter throttle, when wheel-slip had been lessened, yet the car had only been less than 3 m.p.h. slower.

This illustrates the effect which the rough beach had on the machine. If the surface had been smooth, enabling full throttle to be usefully employed, the record figure must have been set very much higher than was actually the case. I was so convinced of this, that I wanted to try again. I had a feeling that, even with the beach in its present condition, the speed could be raised, if the throttle control were employed more carefully than I had been able to do on the second run. Unfortunately, I was completely tired out, and it was not possible to attempt another effort that day; in any case, the ligaments of my left arm had suffered so much that it was painful to hold anything in my left hand, and I could not have gripped the steering-wheel properly.

I considered going out the next day, but the doctor who examined my arm forbade this. As it was, the weather did not improve and, finally, we decided to return home.

The first step towards 300 m.p.h. had been taken, and almost the first question I was asked concerned the possibility of my going on and, if so, where I should make the attempt. I intended to continue but was doubtful whether a future attempt would be made at Daytona or elsewhere. In any case, nothing could be done for some time, because we had learned enough to be able still further to improve the car and bring five miles a minute within definite reach. It was not until nearly two years later, however, that I was able to make a further attempt on the record.

. . . . .

My first consideration in this next attempt was where the car should be run. Despite the kindness I had always received at Daytona, experience had made it clear that the beach could not be relied upon. We now considered a course which offered great possibilities, in view of what had occurred there a year earlier.

This course was the dry Salduro Lake, situated about 125 miles west of Salt Lake City, Utah, where an American driver named 'Ab' Jenkins had set up a series of wonderful long-distance records. The conditions appeared to be as nearly perfect, in some respects, as it was possible to obtain. The surface was formed by encrusted salt, quite smooth and extremely hard; in fact, marking flags could only be inserted by first making a hole with an iron spike. The air was so clear that mountains over a hundred miles away could be seen and, because of the light colour of the lake bed, it never became really dark at night. In a later chapter I give a fuller description of this remarkable track.

At this time, however, we finally decided to go to Daytona instead. *Blue Bird* had now been completely rebuilt and redesigned. In its final form, the chassis still incorporated some parts of the machine which had taken the record at Pendine; the brake-drums, brake shoes and mechanism, the stub-axles and king-pins were from the old car, while we were using the same steering-wheel and chassis side members, with the Rolls-Royce engine employed for 1933.

The radiator was much bigger and occupied almost the full width between the front wheels. As before, the nose of the engine-cover came down behind this, so that no wind could enter the car.

The radiator was provided with a shutter, controlled by a lever in the cockpit; by knocking this lever over, just before entering the mile, the shutter would be closed, thus discounting any resistance which might be offered by wind rushing through the radiator when the car was at the peak of its speed; wind-tunnel tests told us this should give the car an increase of speed of 10 m.p.h.

We abandoned independent wheel fairings and extended the body at the sides, thus forming a fairing between the wheels; these were now enclosed, very much as had been done on the 1,000-h.p. Sunbeam, except that in the case of *Blue Bird*, the tops of the wheels remained exposed.

In order to stop wheel-spin which had affected the car so badly in my previous effort twin rear wheels were fitted. We also introduced a "wind-brake". This was formed by two flaps set on either side of the back axle, and was operated by a vacuum control. These flaps remained horizontal until the brake pedal was used, when they rose to a vertical position, and the resistance which they provided would assist the brakes in slowing down the car.

Blue Bird had been built with the idea of taking the fullest possible advantage of every yard of the

Daytona course. We knew that the car was capable of much more than 300 m.p.h., but it would be unable to reach this rate of travel—owing to the shortness of the course—unless the car attained real speed very quickly. At the same time, speed would have to be reduced more quickly than before, after leaving the mile, otherwise the machine was likely to run beyond the limits of the available beach.

After we had broken the record with 253 m.p.h., I had calculated that two more attempts would be necessary before we could achieve five miles a minute. One of these efforts had already been made, and we had brought the land speed up to 272 m.p.h. Only by good luck could we reach 300 m.p.h. without the second intermediate attempt. It was my opinion, although I wanted to do the higher speed if it was at all possible, that we should be fortunate if this effort in 1935 reached between 285 m.p.h. and 290 m.p.h.

Full success required a perfect beach, and this was the one thing that we could not command. If we were given it, fortune would be treating us more kindly at Daytona than we had ever known before and, in that case, we hoped to be able to make an adequate response.

. . . . .

We arrived at Daytona Beach on the last day of January 1935 and, as on previous occasions, received a magnificent welcome.

During the inevitable delays in making a test run, I spent much time exploring the beach, and decided to duplicate an experiment which we had tried at Verneuk Pan, where we had put down a white line along the centre of the selected course. I had found it of great assistance in keeping straight. The officials agreed to mark the beach with a strip two feet wide, made from a mixture of oil and lampblack.

After two weeks of waiting a test run was possible. In this initial run I did not aim at a record, but the performance of *Blue Bird*, travelling at about 200 m.p.h., provided valuable experience. Another fortnight passed before we made a second run, when the beach was far from perfect, although it did seem just possible that we might beat the record.

Blue Bird went away with a splendid start and, accelerating splendidly, had reached a speed of more than 240 m.p.h. when I suddenly became aware of exhaust fumes in the cockpit. This was alarming, because I had experienced these fumes during a previous attempt, and knew how rapid was their overpowering effect. The fumes were accompanied by scorching heat and, for a moment, I thought that the carburettor had caught fire.

I turned off the petrol and used the air-brake, bringing *Blue Bird* to a stop some three and a half miles farther on, the car having then gone through the measured mile, recording a speed of 233 m.p.h. in spite of the mishap. When we examined the car it was to find that the wind created by the machine's passage had caught the bonnet at one side. The metal panelling had been forced over the exhaust ports, which were cut off level with the bonnet, diverting flames and fumes into the car.

The damage was not sufficient to prevent another run. Once again, however, the engine cover lifted, and again I was forced to slow down, recording only 208·2 m.p.h. But we travelled fast enough to learn that the surface of the beach was such that any attempt to improve upon existing figures was quite out of the question.

I had been strapped into the cockpit, otherwise the bumps would have thrown me out, while the flying sand was even worse than it had been during the first test. I found that sand had smothered the cockpit, clogging my nostrils and ears, while the black line down the course was proved impracticable, largely because the oil which formed its base was flung over my goggles and the windscreen.

Work on the car was carried on throughout the night and, although conditions were still unsatisfactory, I decided, the following day, to have a third try at the record.

After getting off with an excellent start, I went through the forty-foot opening in the pier doing rather more than 130 m.p.h. With the throttle wide open the car roared on, and at 200 m.p.h. I changed to top gear. It was then I began to feel the bumps, because the sand was very uneven, and I realized that I might be asking too much from the car.

As the speed mounted, the bumps became alarming, growing so severe that—in spite of my safety belt—I was bounced up and down in the cockpit. More than once, the top of my head rose above the windscreen, to be caught by a terrific blast of wind. Then, just before we entered the measured mile, there came the worst bump of all. I was shot straight upwards from my seat, catching the wind fairly in the face, so that my goggles were blown downwards, clamping over my nose and mouth.

Blue Bird was then doing fully 270 m.p.h. I could do nothing except grip the steering-wheel and keep the machine straight. I was half-blinded by sand and, owing to the position of the goggles, I could hardly breathe, but I managed to keep my foot hard down on the throttle pedal, because I did not want to spoil the run by slowing up. The length of time occupied by the car in covering the mile seemed an eternity while, because there was no protection for my eyes, I could hardly see more than 200 yards ahead. Fortunately *Blue Bird* remained on her course, and when I had passed the mark at the end of the mile I slowed, ran to the end of the beach and stopped.

The car's speed on that run was registered as 270·473 m.p.h., but I decided that a return run was useless, because the sand was far too rough. The car had been thrown about very badly, and it seemed better to wait a little longer for a good beach, than to make a return trip and risk damaging the machine.

Two days later, another effort appeared possible, but at the last moment—and when the car was actually ready to start—it was decided that the course was unsafe, due to a strong wind that got up suddenly. Then on March 7, we found the beach better than it had been before, and once more *Blue Bird* was rolled down to the sands to make what we all hoped would be a final and successful attack.

· · · · · ·

Visibility was very good when *Blue Bird* arrived on the beach, but wind soon began to rise and a haze drifted in from the sea. Everything was made ready, the engine was started up and *Blue Bird* went off.

Blue Bird accelerated magnificently, but, after cutting the piles of the pier very closely, was checked two or three times by patches of water. With my foot hard down on the throttle pedal, we went into the measured distance. Owing to the bumps near the entrance to the mile, I could not release one hand from the steering-wheel, in order to use the level which closed the radiator shutters and which, we knew, would assist *Blue Bird's* speed by making the nose a solid, streamlined shape. The car kept to her course all through the mile, and I slowed down without difficulty at the far end.

It was evident before *Blue Bird* stopped, that this run had been much more successful than any before, and I was soon informed that we had gone through the mile in 13·2 seconds, which was equivalent to 272·72 m.p.h.—an improvement on the existing record by just about a quarter of a mile an hour against a fairly strong wind. Little as this seems, it was very encouraging to have improved upon the figures against a head wind, and I knew that I should be able to go still faster during the northward run, and so actually beat the record.

We spent twenty minutes in changing tyres, then *Blue Bird* began the return trip, and I soon found myself in trouble. I was now starting from the south end of the beach, and the sand here was very rough indeed, particularly for a mile or so short of the measured distance. This roughness had not been noticeable on the first run, because the car had been slowing down.

I had the throttle wide open, and the start of the mile was well in sight, when *Blue Bird* hit an ugly bump. The car left the ground and leaped through the air for over thirty feet before the wheels touched the sand again; we measured this distance afterwards. As the car weighed nearly five tons, there was a tremendous impact when the machine came down again, and it was this which completely tore the treads from the tyres, while the machine swerved towards the dunes and the soft sand on the inside of the course.

I felt the tail slide outwards, but I straightened the machine and *Blue Bird* went flying on towards the measured mile with fragments of shredded rubber spinning from the wheels. Once again the car swerved, and I now had literally to fight to

[Photo: *Fox Photos Ltd*

Across the dazzling sands of Salt Lake at over 300 m.p.h.

[Photo: *Fox Photos Ltd*

The camera catches an unusual view of the front of Sir Malcolm's *Blue Bird* during refuelling.

[Photo: *The Topical Press Agency Ltd.*

Out of sight but at the wheel of his Railton-Mobil-Special, Mr. John Cobb waits before his attempt on the world's land speed record.

[Photo: *The Topical Press Agency Ltd.*

A view of the Railton-Mobil-Special with the body of the car removed, exposing the chassis.

bring it back to the course, still with full throttle, achieving this just in time to keep clear of the soft sand and to get *Blue Bird* on to the course again; but all the way down the measured mile she was swaying from side to side owing to my having had to wrench the wheel a moment previously. We cleared the distance, and came to a stop near the pier, when I learned that the car had registered 281·03 m.p.h. on this second run. We had thus set up a new record with an average speed of 276·816 m.p.h., the old figures being 272·46 m.p.h.

. . . . .

Blue Bird's time during the fastest of the two runs was 12·81 secs. In order to touch 300 m.p.h., the car would have had to travel through the mile in twelve seconds, so that the machine had actually been within four-fifths of a second of our objective while, on the first trip, it had been one and one-fifth seconds off 300 m.p.h.

It was obvious that the fractions of a second which stood between us and complete success were due entirely to the condition of the beach, and were not the fault of the car. I felt certain that we could still achieve all we wished if only the sands improved sufficiently and, for this reason, we decided to stay on at Daytona. We had created a new

K

record, but we had not done the 300 m.p.h. which I was convinced was possible.

Actual work had brought five miles a minute in sight, and we had waited so long that I felt that it was time we had a little real luck, and I hoped that patience might bring more kindly weather. This hope was a vain one, however. The days slipped past, waiting in vain for a favourable beach; then we decided that it was hopeless, because the beach began to break up completely.

Altogether, we had been at Daytona nearly eight weeks when *Blue Bird* was crated and we started for home. I was disappointed that we had failed to reach 300 m.p.h., but the experience gained had been valuable in many ways.

. . . . .

The experience at Daytona convinced me that the beach there was no longer practicable for the increasing speeds necessitated in future attempts on the land-speed record. Even when the conditions were ideal it was a matter of luck whether the sands would allow a car to produce its maximum speed. For this reason, we decided that we should have to find some other course on which to attempt 300 m.p.h., and it was suggested that we should consider the Bonneville Salt Flats, Utah.

I had heard of this site some time before, but had never seriously investigated its possibilities. After our experiences at Verneuk Pan, in 1929, it had seemed better to meet the known difficulties of a course such as Daytona, rather than attempt the record at some place of which we knew little or nothing at all. Then, as I describe in a later chapter, even if a new course could be found which might offer a better racing track than Daytona, it often was situated in such a remote part of the world that many other factors arose to make it unsuitable.

However, the Salt Flats had recently been used very successfully for long-distance record attempts, and it did not take long to collect a mass of accurate information regarding them. They are set close against a spur of the Rocky Mountains, about 120 miles from Salt Lake City, which is 2,600 miles west of New York. The Flats are formed by the bed of an enormous lake having an area of some 500 square miles; winter rains put the whole of the Flats under water, but this evaporates during the summer, leaving a level layer of salt.

This layer is quite hard, but there are some places on it where damp salt remains near the surface, forming spots which can be cut up and make ruts; this meant that any course there had first to be carefully surveyed and planned to ensure a sound surface all the way. The whole area is traversed by inch-high ridges of very hard salt, which require to be scraped smooth, while the Flats are crossed by a highway and a railroad, which tend to limit the selection of a long length of smooth, suitable salt.

Surveys proved that, in spite of the great area of these Flats, there was only one suitable stretch on which we could hope to achieve 300 m.p.h. This was a strip of about thirteen miles which started close against the road, skimmed a patch of rough salt, and ended at a point where the surface was very soft and was likely to bog the machine if *Blue Bird* ran into it at speed.

Reports and photographs promised a very reasonable chance of success, so *Blue Bird* was tuned up once again and, on August 21, 1935, we sailed for New York, after taking certain precautions to ensure that, should the attempt fail, we would collect reliable data on which to base yet another effort.

It can be understood that when *Blue Bird* was travelling at great speed it was quite impossible for me even to give a glance at the various record gauges which were installed. Had I attempted to do so, taking as I must my eyes off the course itself, it would certainly have affected the speed and might even have caused disaster.

To overcome this difficulty we arranged, in conjunction with the Kodak firm, to have a 9 mm. film camera installed in one of the fairings. This camera was operated by a small electric motor, which I switched on before starting on a run. The camera faced the various gauges of which records were required, and the compartment containing these instruments was light-proof. The results of this scheme were highly successful, providing a mass of most useful information.

In addition, a special accelerometer was fitted, from which we should be able to ascertain the actual amount of power employed in overcoming wind and rolling resistance. If we did not achieve the five miles a minute for which we hoped, we were certain to secure valuable knowledge to ensure that our next attempt would make the result certain instead of a matter of chance.

Arriving in New York, I flew to Utah, reaching the Salt Flats on the last day of August. I am unlikely ever to forget my first impression of the tremendous, dry bed of that prehistoric lake. I had formed the idea of what it was like from descriptions and photographs, but the actuality was far more impressive than anything I had imagined.

I saw the Flats as an endless expanse of glittering white, like a snowfield, but far more harsh to the eyes. The temperature was well above 100 degrees Fahr. and the glare of the sunshine was such that tinted spectacles were an absolute necessity to protect the eyes. The Flats are more than 4,000 feet above sea-level, so that the heat did not seem excessive. The atmosphere was so clear that the mountains, forty or fifty miles away, appeared so close that they seemed to loom above the stretch which had been selected for the attempt.

Blue Bird had preceded my own arrival, and we fixed our headquarters at Wendover, a little village about six miles from the course. This out-of-the-way spot had a railroad depot, some petrol stations and a couple of garages, in the larger of which we placed *Blue Bird*.

The whole of the first day I spent examining the course. I was worried whether the tyres would obtain sufficient grip on the smooth salt, while many of the ridges had not been scraped down sufficiently; although they remained only about half an inch in height, they were certain to set up great vibration in the car, and would prevent the tyres obtaining proper adhesion. The American authorities went over the track again and produced a very satisfactory surface, but for which I am sure we should have met with complete defeat.

In some aspects, this attempt was similar to the one at Verneuk Pan, where I had learned the value of a guide line. By the time that the car arrived, a line had been almost completed, made with oil which showed up well against the white surface.

Blue Bird had been prepared for her first test run by Sunday evening, September 1. Work on the course had been quite completed by then, and we decided to try the car out at daybreak the following morning. In spite of the early hour, and the fact that we were 120 miles from Salt Lake City, a big crowd turned out to watch, and just before dawn *Blue Bird* was towed out of her garage.

On the way to the starting point, we found that salt was picked up by the wheels and became packed tightly against the streamlined fairings, rubbing the tyres. This was something that we had not anticipated, and it brought a risk that, at speed, the jammed salt might lock the front wheels. This chance was obviated and overcome, however, by cutting away the lower part of the fairings and so allowing the salt to fall clear.

There was some delay before we received word

that all was ready for the first run; a difficulty had arisen over the timing apparatus and it was towards nine o'clock before everything was satisfactory. By that time, the heat was intense, and it was fortunate that we had erected awnings—one at either end of the course—which protected the car from the burning sun.

We had decided that the first run should be made from south to north; and there were definite reasons for this. When the car came out at the far side of the measured mile, we should have some six miles in which to pull up, compared with only about five miles at Daytona Beach. But on these salt flats there was not so much rolling resistance, while the rarefied air would also help less in retarding the car, so that even six miles might prove too little.

Even if I was unable to pull the car up, however, it would only run off into soft salt; on the other hand, if I ran from north to south and was unable to stop, the machine would be likely to charge at the embankment which carried the highway across the Flats.

It was suggested that I should keep the speed down to about 180 m.p.h., as the car had not been run at all since its overhaul, after it had returned from Daytona. But I knew that it would be necessary to go faster than this if I were to gain any practical knowledge of the course, and how the car was likely to handle at its maximum speed.

There was, incidentally, no way of telling what was likely to happen during this test. A possibility existed that the wheels would not grip the surface at real speed, and that *Blue Bird* would start to slide, which was likely to provide an uncomfortable experience. However, we were making the trial run in order to learn what would occur, and *Blue Bird* got away to a splendid start. I changed to first speed at 90 m.p.h. and was in top gear at 150 m.p.h., and reached 180 m.p.h. almost before I realized it.

In front of me was the black guide-line, running dead straight across the white and glittering surface. I could not see the line for more than about a hundred yards ahead, so that I appeared continually to be chasing it towards the horizon. The surface was so smooth that the car seemed to skim along, and I could not resist opening out until the revolution-counter showed 2,700 r.p.m., which represented 240 m.p.h and provided the most wonderful experience I have ever had.

The car ran so smoothly that I had no need of the safety straps which held me down to my seat, and which had been so necessary at Daytona. *Blue Bird* behaved magnificently, giving me the impression of skimming across a wide and empty space which might have been on the top of the world. Before I expected it, we had cleared the far end of the measured mile, and I applied the wind-brakes, only to find that they had no appreciable effect in slowing the car. I brought the mechanical brakes into action, wondering whether I should be able to pull up in time and not run over the far end of the course. When I sighted the north shelter, however, we had slowed down sufficiently for me to bring the car round and run it to where the mechanics were waiting.

The car had run very well, the course was so good, and everyone was elated. Other mechanics had followed in a fast touring car, and when we looked *Blue Bird* over we found everything in perfect condition. The car was covered from end to end with salt flakes, so that it looked as if we had been through a snowstorm, but none of it had packed up against the wheels.

With everything in such good order, it was unnecessary to test the machine further. We decided to spend the remainder of the day in checking everything over, and make final arrangements for an attempt. In order to cheat the intense heat we determined to make an even earlier start, and the American Automobile Association officials agreed to have everything ready by six o'clock the following morning.

Long before the sun was up, *Blue Bird* was towed out to the starting-point. Wheels were changed, and the engine was warmed up, after which we had to stand by for the order to go, enduring another of those long and nerve-racking waits which seem always to occur on these attempts. This one was, I understand, caused through a visiting motorist driving over the timing wires, which had been set up overnight; some of them had been broken and the damage took more than an hour to repair.

It was just after seven o'clock when we received the "All Clear!" By that time the sun was high in the sky and was making its presence felt, and it was with considerable relief that I climbed into the cockpit. A few minutes later, we were off.

About a mile ahead of the starting-point was a line of telegraph poles, between two of which I had to drive the car; these presented no difficulty however, because they were spaced well apart. Beyond these, each mile was indicated by a numeral on a large board, showing the distance that remained before entering the measured mile; then, beyond this, more boards showed the distance I had left in which to pull up.

Once the car was moving, my one idea was to achieve real speed as quickly as possible. I remembered to switch on the cinematographic gear as *Blue Bird* roared away, and after that I had no thought other than completing the job. We went up to 100 m.p.h. before changing into second gear, and at 200 m.p.h. I changed to top, with the car getting down to her work as she had never done before.

The needle of the revolution-counter seemed to soar round its dial as the car flew on, with one mile sign shooting up after the other, so that I had hardly passed one before the next appeared and rushed to meet us. The car remained quite steady as we roared on along the apparently endless black line, with the wind rushing past and its note rising to a scream.

I had decided to close the radiator shutter when I reached a point two miles short of the measured distance, and as this board whipped into sight I gave one last glance at the revolution-counter. The needle was rising above 3,200 r.p.m., showing that we were then doing 290 m.p.h. and still accelerating. I reached for the lever controlling the radiator shutter, knocked it forward and, immediately, my troubles began.

At once, a film of oil spread over the windscreen, becoming more and more opaque with every second. At the same time, exhaust gases from the engine rushed into the cockpit, growing worse and worse as we neared the timing tapes. I crossed them with the throttle wide open, by which time it was not easy to see the black guide line. Halfway through the mile—which was barely ten seconds later—the fumes began to have their effect. I became aware of ugly shooting pains in my head, reminiscent of those I had experienced before at Daytona, and I knew there was a risk that I should lose consciousness or become dazed and allow the car to run out of control.

I could only just see the black line immediately in front of the car, but I knew that relief would come once I had cleared the mile, when I could ease up. I watched for the red banners at the far end and, after what now seemed to be an age, picked them up. They flashed by almost at once, when I eased the throttle pedal as rapidly as I dared. I could not see the black line at all now, and realized that I had gone off it but, with the throttle closing, fumes no longer came into the cockpit and my head began to clear.

I applied the wind-brakes, then, looking for the guide-line, sighted it to the right. I eased the car towards it, when the near-side front tyre suddenly burst and the machine swerved the other way; we were travelling at well over 280 m.p.h. at the time. *Blue Bird* responded at once when I corrected the skid, but we snaked for some time before I fully regained control and the car steadied. Because of the burst tyre, the steering became heavier and heavier with each moment that passed, while bits of the tyre flew high into the air.

It was necessary to pull up as quickly as possible now, and I used the mechanical brakes. Our speed was then very high, and I remember wondering if the near-side wheel would stand up to the tremendous punishment that it must be receiving. While this was in my mind I saw that the burst tyre had caught fire, and was spinning in a haze of smoke.

After that, I braked heavily. The car remained straight, and stopped about half a mile short of the shelter where mechanics were waiting at the north end of the course. They did not know what had happened, or why I had stopped there, but came out in a hurry when I stood up in my seat and waved to them, after which I attacked the burning tyre with a fire extinguisher.

Some delay followed, because they had to bring out spare wheels, jacks and the starting apparatus for the engine, and make preparations for the return trip. It took about half an hour to change the wheels and make things ready, while more time was lost in clearing the windscreen of the oil film and in cleaning my specially tinted goggles.

During this time, a motor-cyclist arrived to advise me that our speed through the mile had been over 304 m.p.h., which was very good news indeed. We had actually achieved over 300 m.p.h., but had to make a return run at a similar figure in order to establish the record at the speed we had set out to attain. It was obvious that the tyres had received a very severe test, and I wondered if they would stand up to the gruelling work of the second journey. We could find this out only by making the attempt.

The engine was restarted and I was all set to go when a message arrived that the timing wires had broken again and were being repaired. Only fifteen minutes of the hour remained (an hour being the maximum interval allowed by the regulations between the two official runs), and this valuable time slipped past as I sat in the cock-pit, with the car standing in the full glare of the sun. The wait which now followed was the most trying that I have ever known; if the full hour elapsed, that first run would count for nothing.

While I waited, I decided that I would not close the radiator shutter at all. I did not want another experience with those exhaust fumes, and there was a grave risk that, following upon what had already occurred, their effect might be more rapid and more serious. I felt, also, that *Blue Bird* might just reach 300 m.p.h. without the assistance of the closed shutter.

We had five minutes left when I was told that the course was cleared and that the timing apparatus was again in good order. At first the engine would not start; but we eventually got her going and immediately had *Blue Bird* away, after one last moment of apprehension in case the engine should stall and still more time be lost.

Once more we were really moving. I kept glancing at my front tyres, and as we were reaching about 280 m.p.h. I observed an extraordinary thing. The centrifugal force of the spinning front wheels was so great that it made the tyre-treads seem pointed and, apparently, transparent with every turn of the wheels; the tyres were being elongated to an ellipse, full proof of the terrific strain they had to endure.

I took one last glance at the tyres when we were

[Photo: *Fox Photos Ltd*

The 3,000 h.p. Mercédès-Benz, found at Stuttgart, with which the Germans hoped to realise a speed of 450 m.p.h.

[Photo: *Central Press Agency Ltd.*

Captain George Eyston's 5,000 h.p., six-wheeled, eight-tyred monster car photographed in London before leaving for the U.S.A. in 1937.

[Photo: *Central Press Photos Ltd.*

Before his attempt on the water speed record Sir Malcolm Campbell poses obligingly for photographers.

[Photo: *Fox Photos Ltd.*

Another strange view of Captain Eyston's mammoth racing car, from which it was hoped 400 m.p.h. could be obtained.

[Photo: *Central Press Photos Ltd.*

Before taking *Blue Bird II* to Lake Coniston, Sir Malcolm did several trials with a jet-powered speedboat on the Italian Lakes.

nearing 290 m.p.h., just before we arrived at the start of the measured mile. I came to the conclusion that those tyres provided one of the most unpleasant sights I have ever seen; then I forgot about them under the necessity of taking *Blue Bird* as fast as possible over the mile.

This time, we seemed to cover the distance in a flash—the actual time proved to be 12·08 seconds—and once I had passed the banners at the far end, remembered the embankment ahead, and knew that the necessity for pulling up very quickly was more urgent than it had been during the first run. Because of this, I eased the throttle pedal much more rapidly than I should have done, with the result that the tail came round in what was almost a broadside skid.

Fortunately, *Blue Bird* responded when I corrected the slide, at a time when the car was moving at fully 280 m.p.h. As we came out of the skid, I used the mechanical brakes. I could feel their power and the way they checked the car, but I was not sure that we could pull up in time. I was still in doubt when I saw the line of telegraph poles and sighted the embankment. I was making ready to swing the car off the course and run level with the obstruction, when I judged we should be just able to stop. Actually, the car checked about one hundred yards short of the embankment, which was a very narrow margin when one considers the unpleasant situation which would have been created had the brakes failed.

When *Blue Bird* had been run under the shelter and I climbed out, we were given a very enthusiastic reception. I felt sure that this second run had been made at something so close to 300 m.p.h. that the mean speed would be over that figure.

The shelter was linked by a telephone line to that occupied by the timing officials near the measured mile. There was a long wait before any news came through. In the end we were told that the second run had been achieved at a speed of 299·9 m.p.h., which meant that our speed for the record worked out at something very close to 302 m.p.h.

This was great news, but we had hardly time to show our elation before a correction arrived. We were told that there had been a misunderstanding, and that the speed of 299·9 m.p.h. was that of the average for both runs, and that the second trip had registered only about 296 m.p.h.

This news was a very great disappointment. Of course, we had broken the old record, but it appeared that we had been barred from our goal by only one-tenth of a mile per hour. Obviously, we could try again, but nothing could be done just then because, apart from anything else, I found myself left with a splitting headache, caused by the poisonous fumes I had inhaled.

I told the A.A.A. officials that we would try again next morning. *Blue Bird* was towed back to the garage at Wendover and, a little later, we examined the car in order to find out why the closing of the radiator shutter had brought such unpleasant results. We found that this action caused fumes to drift up from the crankcase breather, sucked up into the cockpit by the rush of air past the open top, bringing an oil-mist with it.

We saw that if a covered top were made for the cockpit any possible suction would at once be negatived, while the whole car would become perfectly streamlined and its speed would be increased, possibly by as much as ten or fifteen miles an hour.

Within two hours of our return to Wendover, mechanics began to beat an aluminium panel to form the covered top. They had started work when I was asked to have a word with the A.A.A. officials. I found them very concerned, and they informed me that they had discovered a slight error in their calculations, as a result of which the actual speed for the second run was 298·013, thus giving us a mean speed of 301·1292 m.p.h. for the record.

We had, therefore, actually accomplished all that we had set out to do, but I felt that I would much rather try again the next day and, as it were, make a clean job of it. When I suggested this, they pointed out that the mistake which had been made was so apparent that it would have been discovered when they checked up their figures—as, indeed, had occurred—and that no useful purpose could be served by going out again, since we had done all that we had set out to achieve.

In this way, then, and after so many efforts, we reached our goal of over 300 m.p.h., but that first disappointment out on the Flats had, somehow, robbed us all of much of the pleasure which the achievement should have brought. All that is past, however, and we still have the memory of that magnificent 304 m.p.h. which was the car's highest speed on the first run, while our 301·13 m.p.h. stands as a record achieved by the last of the long line of *Blue Bird's* successes.

The car was capable of even higher speeds. With that covered cockpit and a still longer course, I believe *Blue Bird* could have reached 320 m.p.h.

at least, but the car will not run again. I certainly should like, just once more, to experience the thrill of *Blue Bird* moving under full throttle, and that grand feeling which comes when a new record has been gained and an objective reached. As I have said, it is not easy to give it all up, but one can only regard the necessity as philosophically as possible and accept the fact that, in time, all things must come to an end.

In closing this chapter, I should like to thank Leo Villa and Harry Leech and those other mechanics who stood by me during this work. They are still with me engaged on my work with speed-boats. I must also express my appreciation of the help that I received from the Dunlop firm, upon whose research depended the tyres which served *Blue Bird* so well. There are many, many other friends to whom my thanks are due, and without whose willing aid we could have achieved nothing.

VI

SIX MILES A MINUTE

DURING the next two years I was able to retain the land-speed record of 301·13 m.p.h. I knew, however, that it could be only a question of time before others would attempt to raise it. The first man to do so was Captain George Eyston who, in the winter of 1937, raised the record to 312 m.p.h. with his car, *Thunderbolt*.

It was while I was at Bonneville Salt Flats during my last speed-record attempt that Eyston arrived with another car. His object was to contest a number of long-distance records, and his car for this purpose was *Speed of the Winds*. This machine weighed about two tons, and was specially built for the work that it had to do. To such an extent was it specialized that precautions were taken to shield the exhaust pipes, so that when the car was running through the night the driver would not see the flames that gush from them; this would have dazzled him. One important innovation was the substitution of front-wheel for rear-wheel drive, thus demonstrating in practice an old theory among designers, many of whom suggest that it is easier to pull than to push. There have been many other front-wheel-drive cars, but *Speed of the Winds* was the first of its size.

Captain Eyston has probably broken more records than any other man in the world, and the French have given him the title of "record-man". He was the first to do 100 m.p.h. in a "baby" racing-car—that is a machine with an engine of under 750 c.c., and one which is generally known as a 7-h.p. car. Not satisfied with this, he actually covered 100 miles in sixty minutes in one of these little machines; then he performed the feat of making the car do 120 m.p.h.

Although he is physically a big man, Eyston has a very quiet voice and an equally quiet manner. No one would guess, without knowing it, that he is a wonderfully clever engineer as well as being a racing man. He is one of those drivers who will not allow themselves to take what they regard as an unnecessary risk; that is to say, he will not try to force a car beyond its capabilities. When he makes a record attempt he knows what the machine should be able to do, and he does his utmost to get that speed out of it. If the machine fails he finds out why, and then tries again. This may rightly suggest that he combines science and sure knowledge with his driving ability.

He has competed in many events on the Continent and within the British Isles, while, of course, he was one of the best-known drivers at Brooklands. At Bonneville Salt Flats he made an attack upon the one-hour and the twenty-four-hour records. Assisted by two relief drivers, and driving round a great circular course marked out on the salt, he kept his big car going for a day and a night, averaging 140·5 m.p.h. for the entire twenty-four hours and collecting many other records during the run. He also succeeded in covering 159·3 miles in one hour with the same car—that is, he did not simply touch this speed, he kept it up for a full sixty minutes.

Thunderbolt, with which Eyston successfully attacked my record, was a huge car (I have unfortunately to use the past tense, for this car was destroyed by fire in New Zealand, early in 1947. *Speed of the Winds*, likewise, no longer exists, for it was lost in the London blitz). It was engined by two 3,000-h.p. Rolls-Royce engines, geared together, and the whole car weighed six tons. At top speed its consumption of petrol was five gallons a minute. It was fitted with coil springs and air-brakes.

It is rather terrifying to consider what such a monster car could do if the driver was to lose control while travelling at, say, 330 m.p.h. Weighing six times as much as a 12-in. shell and only twenty-five per cent slower, *Thunderbolt* could tear its way through the armour-plated side of a great battleship. It could go right through the Empire State Building in New York. Striking a small hillock on the course, it could leap over Snowdon or could run 3,000 feet up a vertical wall. Shooting off Southend Pier at that speed, it would travel three-quarters of a mile before it hit the water.

Every mile an hour above 300 presented a scientific problem. The same is true with man's next efforts over 400 m.p.h. As the speed goes up the difficulties increase out of all proportion. One difficulty that Eyston had to face, for instance, was in connection with breathing and physical endurance. In his first successful attempt on the record he found it exceedingly difficult to strike a balance between having enough air in the cockpit to breathe and keeping the interior free from carbon monoxide. At the same time he had to give himself sufficient protection in the cockpit to keep his goggles from being torn off.

In his second attempt, in 1938, when Eyston raised the speed record to 345·5 m.p.h., *Thunderbolt* had an all-enclosed cockpit. It was scientifically ventilated, but even then the driver wore a special fresh-air mask to prevent himself being asphyxiated by the deadly fumes which, with many thousands of horse-power, were produced in sufficient quantities to poison several men.

This great car was thirty-five feet long, about seven feet six inches broad, and about four feet high. It had an enormous radiator in front; though not very big in area, there were 16,000 tubes for the two engines. The whole car was built on a surface plate about thirty feet long, and all measurements were from that surface plate, so that there was little difficulty in seeing that the job was properly lined up. After the car was properly completed it was possible to take it all to pieces and build it up again in about forty-eight hours—if you knew how!

In setting up a new record of 345 m.p.h. Eyston beat his own previous record by a large margin. *Thunderbolt* was painted black to overcome the glaring sun, which robbed him of the record in an attempt made three days previously. On that occasion the timing trap failed, owing to the excessively bright sunlight affecting the photo-electric cell of the "electric eye".

Eyston's record was not allowed to stand for

long. Following on his footsteps to the Bonneville Salt Flats was John Cobb and his Napier-Railton car. Cobb was no stranger to the Flats, for, like Eyston, he had raced there before, in 1935, when within a week he had captured twenty-one world's records, only to lose many of them to his rival.

Reid Railton who designed Cobb's car turned out one of the most beautiful pieces of British design, engineering and workmanship that have ever been created. This designer had been responsible for my *Blue Bird* and also assisted in designing the motor-boat *Blue Bird*, which holds the world's water-speed record.

Reid Railton probably knows more about designing for high speeds than any other man in England. Shy, spectacled, modest, he shuns the limelight. When he has to get on his feet and talk about his achievements he always says that he "really had very little to do with it".

He is not only a brilliant engineer, but he has made an extensive study of the effects of air resistance and its reduction by streamlining. The ingenuity with which he has applied sound and proved orthodox methods of construction in a totally unorthodox way to the design of Cobb's car is astonishing.

For instance: In order to achieve the most perfect streamlining possible, projections from the smooth skin of the body must be kept to a minimum. Even the use of hinged or movable panels covering fuel, oil and water-filler pipes, or to get access to the engines is bad, for their edges increase skin friction. So Railton designed the body all in one piece, constructed so that it is attached to eight outriggers on the chassis and can be lifted off bodily by six mechanics.

Shaped like a great inverted slipper, twenty-nine feet long by eight feet wide by four feet high, this car is made of the thinnest aluminium alloy sheathing, and weighs under 500 lbs.

Here is another example of his ingenuity. If you are going to cool a car like this by orthodox means you have to use a radiator. There must be some way for air to get to the radiator and that means another break in the streamlining. So Railton did away with the radiator altogether and slung a seventy-five-gallon tank on the near side of the chassis to balance the oil and fuel tank on the other side. This tank was filled with ice before each run, and the water to keep it cool circulated through the ice.

Then Railton had to face the problem of getting the two big 1,450-h.p. engines with their superchargers and transmission gear into the least possible space, and to support their ton of weight in the chassis. So he set them at angles to the centre-line of the car, their transmission shaft driving the axles through bevel gears. To get the length which would accommodate gear-boxes, clutches and transmission brakes, he had the engine at the rear driving the front wheels, the engine at the front driving the back wheels. And he supported them on cantilevers on an S-shaped box-girder, the engines themselves forming the strengthening members of the cantilevers.

In order to get the necessary sweep of tail for the streamlining he wanted, Railton crab-tracked the car, that is, set the rear wheels closer together than the front. The track of the front wheels was five feet six inches, that of the rear only three feet six inches.

It was only a fortnight after Eyston had made his world record of 345·5 m.p.h. that John Cobb set out to beat it. At his first attempt he failed by less than a tenth of a second, largely owing to the damp salt and an adverse wind. On his second attempt he was more fortunate. On his first run, Cobb achieved the record speed of 353·29 m.p.h.—which meant eight miles faster than Eyston's record. On the return run the speed was slower at 347·6 m.p.h., but it gave a mean speed of 350·2 m.p.h.

So had passed one more landmark in the history of speed on wheels.

Even this record was to last only one day. For, twenty-four hours later, Captain Eyston established yet another record with an average speed of 357·5 m.p.h. Cobb made no further attempt at the time to defeat this last record, but when he returned the following year (1939) he succeeded in raising the speed record considerably to the figure of 369·7 m.p.h.—the first time that six miles a minute had been officially attained by motor-car, and forty years exactly after Jenatzy had driven at a mile a minute.

Cobb's attempts on the record were all the more remarkable because, until he took the car to Utah, he had never before driven at more than 180 m.p.h.

It was during Eyston's last attempt that he had a narrow escape from disaster, from which he was only saved by his magnificent driving and presence of mind.

He went out in order to try and beat Cobb's record speed. *Thunderbolt* was streaking up to the measured mile at about 360 m.p.h. when the right-hand back end seemed to collapse.

Keeping his head in the coolest possible way,

Eyston managed to avoid crashing into the dense masses of spectators, and brought the wobbling monster to a standstill three miles from the end of the twelve-mile course after it had ploughed deep trenches in the iron-hard salt.

The tyres had become entangled in the cowling, which, in turn, had caused the cowling to become entangled in a wheel, and so bad was the damage that repairs could not be carried out on the spot. It was bad luck, for there was no doubt that he was travelling faster at the time of the mishap than he had ever travelled before. Twisted and torn, *Thunderbolt* was shipped back to England.

. . . . .

I conclude this account of attempts on the world's motor-car speed record with John Cobb's magnificent performance at Bonneville Salt Flats. There, on September 16, 1947, driving his Railton car, he raised his own previous record from 369 m.p.h. to over 394 m.p.h. and achieved a one-way speed of over 400 m.p.h.

These figures represent one of the biggest single forward steps ever taken in the history of the land-speed record; a fact particularly creditable in view of the mathematical laws governing high-speed travel. No other country has built a car which will compare in speed with the British effort, for the Railton was conceived and built in Britain in its entirety.

The car was originally designed in 1937 and used in Cobb's previous successful attempts. It was built with two Napier-Lion engines designed during the 1914–18 war. It was first run during September 1938, achieving a speed then of 342 m.p.h., and it has not yet reached the extreme limit of its capacity.

The whole cycle of Cobb's record run in one direction took approximately 200 seconds, which were approximately equally disposed between the periods of positive and negative acceleration. Within ten seconds the car was travelling at 100 m.p.h.; 200 m.p.h. was obtained in fifty seconds; and 300 m.p.h. in seventy seconds. Braking down from 400 m.p.h. to a halt took about 100 seconds.

John Cobb's performance shows that his British car is now 127 m.p.h. faster than any non-British car, and 187 m.p.h. faster than any car ever constructed in the United States of America. That is something we can well be proud of.

VII

THE WORK OF DRIVING AT HIGH SPEEDS

THERE is a popular idea that the racing-driver is a man who puts his foot hard down on the throttle pedal right from the start, and keeps his car travelling recklessly until the race is over.

This is quite wrong. A man who handled his car in this way would be likely to find himself out of any race, and this includes attempts on speed records, long before it was over, if nothing worse happened to him.

This was brought home to me in my first big race, which was one of the famous 200-mile events once held at Brooklands. In the 1923 race I managed to secure the wheel of one of the finest racing-machines of those days. This was a Fiat, of a type which had been extremely successful in Continental road work. An Italian driver named Salamano had entered a similar machine, and the fact that these two cars were running in the event created a great deal of excitement.

Both machines had "blowers", which is a term often used by racing men for "superchargers". The supercharger is a device which "blows" more petrol vapour and air into the cylinders than the engine itself would normally draw. Within reason, the more explosive mixture you can get into the cylinders, the more power the engine gives off. Fitted with a supercharger, an engine becomes about one-third more powerful than without one, the whole car being very specially built for racing.

These two magnificent red-painted Fiats were the first supercharged machines to be seen at the track, and many people thought that they could not fail to win the race. In fact, it seemed so certain that either Carlo Salamano or myself would win that we made a private arrangement about it. It was agreed that whoever held the lead at the end of the first lap should retain it until ten laps from the end, and over the final ten laps we were to fight the issue out between ourselves.

The year 1923 is a very long time ago, and I had a great deal to learn about motor-racing; it is a subject concerning which it is always possible to learn something new. Salamano was a very experienced driver, and it seemed impossible that I could have much chance against him. He was, of course, most friendly, and helped me all that he could before the race; but I knew that once the flag fell it would be a case of the better man winning.

On an October afternoon the cars were sent away, with Salamano making use of all the tremendous acceleration of his machine and streaking immediately into the lead. I was so eager to get going that I made a very bad start and stalled my engine; in consequence, I was left behind while all the rest streaked off. Mechanics soon restarted the car, and I drove flat out the moment I got going, with the result that I was driving close behind the Italian driver at the end of the second lap, all the other cars in the race falling steadily farther behind us.

We were lapping at about 100 m.p.h., and the superiority of the two Fiats was such that there was no need to go any faster. I expected Salamano to ease the pace a little, so that the two machines would run easily through the race until the last ten laps. Salamano, however, increased his speed, until we were moving at least 10 m.p.h. more quickly than the fastest of the other machines.

In order to remain with him I had to keep the throttle wide open. If I had slowed he would have gone well ahead, and I should have had no chance to race against him in the final duel. I had been told before the race that the Fiat engines would stand up to any speed we asked from them. Even so, Brooklands track was very hard on a car, and, as I realized later, I should have eased up. As it was, I accepted Salamano's pace, and by the end of a dozen laps we were a full lap ahead of the next machine—and it was there that the Italian suddenly slowed down.

I shot past, easing up a little, watching for him as I came round again. I saw his car halted and smoking, and almost at the same time I heard a noise from my own engine. Soon afterwards the noise increased and the engine stopped, while the cockpit was filled with smoke.

I coasted on to the pits, there to discover that I had broken a connecting rod, while Salamano had suffered a similar fate.

The two Fiats were thus out of the race, so that the slower cars went roaring triumphantly past us. If the two Italian machines had been driven more cautiously they would have lasted the race, and one of them would almost certainly have won. As it was, they had been driven flat out from the start, and bitterly did Salamano and myself pay the penalty of our speed. Salamano, for his part, had never raced on a track before, and did not altogether realize that, without bends and turns which slow a machine, it was possible to ask too much from a car; while I, of course, simply did not know enough.

The incident serves to illustrate the fact that a racing-car must be handled very carefully and considerately. It is a very highly tuned piece of mechanism, and ought to be driven no faster than is absolutely necessary. An athlete who is running in a five-mile event never wins if he goes all out from the start. If he holds the lead towards the finish, he then runs only as fast as is necessary to keep off any challengers. A motor-race is really no different, so far as the drivers are concerned.

It may, I think, be of interest to explain how a racing-car is handled. A short dash at speed down an open road is one thing; the concentrated effort needed to drive a specially-built and extremely costly racing-car, such as *Blue Bird*, all out for an attempt on the world's speed record is another. A different type of technique is required.

A flair for high-speed driving is obviously the most essential requirement in the driver who seeks a world record. He must possess a very quick-acting brain to cope with the emergencies that constantly arise. In the previous chapters I have illustrated, on several occasions, how instantaneous decisions have meant the difference between life and death, success and failure.

There are some men who combine real engineering ability with driving skill, but they are few. The designer creates the car, and the mechanics build and look after it. The driver's job is simply to get the best possible performance out of the machine, but he should be part and parcel of it. Of course, the more the driver knows the more helpful he can be to the mechanics and others who tune or design his car; but his real job is to drive the machine and take the risks involved.

He will certainly go and look at the machine while it is being made ready; he will have his measurements taken for the cockpit, so that it can be built to fit him. No driver wants too much room in his cockpit; if there is he will be thrown about and his shoulders will be bruised by the squab and the sides. If it is too restricted he will be cramped, and few things are worse. There are other small individual details which will help him feel at home in the car.

Motor-racing is a very arduous test of physical stamina. If he is to do justice to himself and his car he must be extremely fit, with nerves and muscles as well tuned as his machine. The physical and nervous strain is tremendous, and cannot possibly be sustained by a man who is not in the best of condition. If he is not fit he certainly does not get the best out of the car, and is much more liable at some moment of crisis to make a wrong decision.

A driver must therefore be fit, and before a race he does nothing which will spoil his condition. In fact, he takes almost as much care of himself as a man entering for an Olympic contest. If he smokes at all it is very little, and wines and spirits are best left alone until the race is over.

Perhaps the most important thing the driver has to keep constant sight of is to avoid any accident. Quite apart from the fact that an accident when travelling at great speed may result in injury or death to himself, there is the certainty that the machine will be damaged and repairs may be very expensive. Also—and this is important—the car may well lose its chance of breaking the record, especially if extensive repairs are required. Somehow a machine is rarely the same after it has been severely damaged, no matter how carefully the repairs are carried out.

A driver can cause great damage to his car without outwardly appearing to have had an accident; he can over-drive it and blow up, and so wreck the engine. In other words—surprising as this may seem—he can drive his car too fast.

In order that this shall be made quite clear it must be explained that every racing-car has what is known as a "revolution-counter"; this takes the place of the speedometer on an ordinary machine. As everyone knows, an engine has pistons which travel up and down; connecting rods link these to a crankshaft which, under the action of the pistons, turns round and round. In this way the up-and-down motion of the pistons is changed to a rotary movement, and every complete turn which they give to the crankshaft is called a "revolution". Because of this an engine is said to "turn" or "revolve", and the revolution-counter simply counts the number of times that the crankshaft is spun round, usually calculated as "revolutions per minute"—r.p.m.

It may be as well to add that the turning motion of the crankshaft is carried through the gear-box and along a propeller shaft to the back axle, which actually spins the wheels. If the crankshaft is turning slowly, then the rear wheels also turn slowly; the faster the engine revolves the faster the wheels turn—and the greater the speed of the car. From this one may understand that the reading on the revolution-counter is very like that of a speedometer, and a car's speed can be calculated from it.

A racing-driver, however, is not really interested in his machine's speed as such, and he never knows accurately how fast he is travelling in miles per hour. When, for instance, *Blue Bird* was travelling over the Bonneville Salt Flats, in Utah, working up pace for an attack on the land-speed record, and the revolution-counter showed 3,200 r.p.m., I knew that the car was travelling at about 280 m.p.h.; the car *might* actually have been doing only 270 m.p.h., losing pace through wheel-spin. I had to work the engine revolutions up to 3,500 r.p.m. in order to get the car travelling at over 300 m.p.h., and the actual speed in miles per hour was recorded by timing apparatus beside the course.

Blue Bird was driven according to the revolution-counter. I knew only the pace at which the car should have been travelling according to the position of the needle against its dial, and not until I was told afterwards did I know just exactly how fast the machine had gone.

Blue Bird has a very big Rolls-Royce engine, capable of developing 2,500 horse-power, and this engine cannot naturally turn over so rapidly as smaller racing motors, although its piston speed is very high. These smaller machines have engines which get up to anything from 6,000 to 8,500 r.p.m., and a driver who is on top gear with this reading on his revolution-counter knows when his engine is developing its full quota of power. He also knows that if he maintains this engine-speed indefinitely he will be over-driving the machine, and that something is likely to fail in his engine. And in this lies the true reason for the revolution-counter.

These revolution-counters are divided into sections painted different colours. This variety of colours prevents mistakes being made regarding the engine revolutions, for the quickest glance can tell, for instance, that when the dial indicates a green sector that will mean, say, 5,000 r.p.m., while a red sector represents 6,000 r.p.m.

Wheel-spin, of course, is a factor which can make considerable difference to the apparent speed. At Daytona, for instance, I have seen the revolution-counter of *Blue Bird* showing 4,000 r.p.m., which was equivalent to about 330 m.p.h., although I knew that the car was only travelling at about 280 m.p.h. This loss in speed was due entirely to excessive wheel-spin, caused through the rough condition of the beach at the time.

On the other hand, when running at high speeds

over a perfectly even surface such as is found on the Bonneville Salt Flats, wheel-spin does not take place, and as the tyres become elliptical (as I have described in a former chapter), consequently the speed is greater than that shown on the reading of the engine revolution-counter.

One of the most important items in a racing-driver's kit is the broad belt he wears about his waist. It is fastened quite tightly, and its object is to help him to withstand the bumps which any racing-machine inflicts when it is running. Because of his speed the driver must sustain a succession of jolts, and unless he had something to support him he would dissipate a great deal of strength and nervous energy in bracing his body. The abdominal belt helps him, while, apart from anything else, it prevents him from feeling sick as a result of the bumps. Everyone knows the feeling of nausea which comes as the result of continued jolting.

Goggles or a visor form another essential for speed-racing, and a "crash" helmet, which will protect the head in case of accident. Specially-made driving gloves, with no fingers to them while the backs are formed of netted cord, and the palms are very soft and pliable, are necessary. They are held in position by elastic bands at the wrist, and are comfortable to wear; the driver's hands are saved from the friction of the steering-wheel and from being bruised by the gear lever. For shoes the driver adopts something very light and easy-fitting; this is because down by the pedals is the hottest part of the cockpit.

. . . . .

I am often asked if there is any sensation of speed when one is tucked down in a racing-car. Most definitely there is, possibly more than when one is taking part in a road-race with its need for braking for corners and swerving to pass other cars. One of my most intense sensations of speed in a world record attempt was at Pendine Sands, a beach on which I was the first to set up record runs.

At the time I was trying to capture the 150 m.p.h. record and I started off with some sensation of adventure. My chief driving concern, after I had changed into top gear, was to keep my foot on the throttle pedal, so that I had to brace myself in the seat all the time, to be sure that the throttle was held wide open owing to the bad surface of the course.

The sense of speed was intense, yet quite unaccompanied by any attendant indication of danger. The marking flags rushed to meet me instead of, as at more moderate speeds, appearing to be approached by the car. The beach raced away beneath the front of the machine, while spray and sand was flung like a curtan high in the rear, almost hiding the car from the excited watchers.

The pressure on my ear-drums was very heavy, and the air, droning past, felt solid, very much as water feels when one is coming to the surface after a steep dive. I was conscious of the bumps and little patches of soft sand occasionally checking the car; when this happened, wet sand slashed upwards from the front wheels, so that my goggles were obscured before the end of each run, making vision extremely difficult. All this was due to the fact that there was little protection in the cockpit from the elements.

This problem of wet and soft sand was one of the greatest handicaps in driving for the earlier land-speed records. But a far worse accident happened on the practically perfect surface of Brooklands. I include an account of this experience, not so much to retell of a lucky escape, as to illustrate one of the sudden, unexpected happenings of speed driving.

My mechanic, Leo Villa, and I were practising with a Bugatti which I had bought, and were out to improve the carburation. We covered several laps, stopping frequently to lift the bonnet to make further adjustments. Following the usual racing practice, this bonnet was secured by two straps, one at the front, the other at the back. Our periodical tinkerings brought much improvement in the machine which began to run very well indeed.

I was watching the revolution-counter as I drove. I could see the dial through the spokes of the steering-wheel and, at the same time, I was able to look along the bonnet and keep the track in view. Driving like this, we swung down off the banking to the railway straight at around 110 m.p.h. when, without the least warning, the bonnet lifted, forced upward by the thrust of the wind. The strap at the front had apparently not been secured at our last stop, the buckle slipped, while the second strap stayed put, acting like a hinge.

The bonnet rose and slammed completely over, catching me squarely across the head. This happened so suddenly that I was unable to protect my head with my hand. This bonnet was a heavy thing, backed by the force of wind amounting to a 110-m.p.h. gale, and the force with which it struck me was terrific.

I was knocked completely unconscious in an instant.

That was inevitable. It is necessary, however, to explain it because of what followed. Although I was definitely knocked out, insensibility lasted for only a second. I came round again at once, my mind working with one clear thought. This was to keep the car straight and bring it to a halt; the only alternative being certain death for both of us.

When my eyes opened, the track ahead was masked by the still forced-up bonnet which was jammed over my head. I was aware of Villa trying desperately to lift this cover clear, but this was impossible, for, owing to the wind pressure and its weight, it was beyond his strength. So, jammed down in my seat, all I could see was through a narrow slit directly in front of me where the bonnet curved over the scuttle-dash. It was no more than the merest slit which gave me a very constricted view of the track. Still it was just enough to enable me to keep the car straight, while I slammed on the brakes as hard as I could.

I felt the Bugatti slow right down—then everything went black again.

When I came round again, I found I had been carried into the paddock for attention after the car had skidded to a halt broadside across the track. But of that, and my fight to keep it straight after the cover hit me, I had not the slightest recollection. I did not even remember taking the car out, or of the practice spins, or the hit on the head.

Only as several days went by, however, did recollection begin to filter back little by little. But it was some eight weeks later before I regained a complete—and most vivid—memory of every detail of that almost tragic ride.

These incidents from my own experiences illustrate some of the conditions which a driver has to face. They have all been real experiences—not something one could have gleaned from a book. They show, I think, the necessity for the successful driver to possess that extraordinary instinct of sympathy with mechanism which enables him to appreciate and understand each little characteristic of the car he happens at the moment to be driving. There must be unity between the two.

I could point to no clearer example of unity between driver and machine than the driving of London buses. I have often watched with amazement the feats of skill and daring which some of the drivers perform in the most crowded thoroughfares. It is not an easy matter to take a bulky bus through London's congested traffic, but when this

[*Autocar* photograph

It was in 1935 that Sir Malcolm Campbell won the world's Land Speed Record at Bonneville Salt Flats, America.

[Photo: *Central Press Photos*

Another design of a jet-engine speedboat with which Sir Malcolm hoped to reach new speeds on water.

[Photo: *Central Press Photos Ltd.*

Colonel "Goldie" Gardner with the tiny machine he used for his attempt on the speed record for cars up to 500 c.c.

feat is performed at a speed of twenty miles an hour or even more, the skill in driving is sufficiently marked to arouse praise. Hundreds of times daily the driver has to think instantaneously what action he must take to secure the safety of his bus and its passengers. One moment of hesitation and the moment for action would be past.

Allied to this need of unity, of sympathy between driver and machine, is good judgment. That, again, is a matter of temperament. You either possess this special instinct, or you don't.

One final word in regard to the special qualities in connection with the successful driving of a racing-car. The general rule applies that the driver must know his car. If this rule is important in the driving of an ordinary touring-car, it is doubly important when the car is built for speed, and for the taking of risks with the sole idea of covering a mile in a still shorter period of time than has ever been accomplished previously on wheels. A mistake at five miles a minute or faster has no opportunity of being rectified. There must be no ignorance of the power of the brakes or the skidding propensities of the car, and brutality in handling would end in disaster. A racing-car, like a racehorse, must be nursed through. If the strenuous nature of an attempt on a record demands that everything must be risked, then the driver knows what he is risking, and a breakage or an accident is not always unexpected. The art lies in obtaining and maintaining the very utmost speed over every yard of the distance, with at the same time the least possible strain on the car.

In driving in a speed attempt, the great idea is to keep going and to allow nothing to dishearten or discourage. It is the driver who is always "pushing on"—meeting his troubles, overcoming them, and no matter how annoying or serious delays may be, getting going as soon as possible, wasting not a moment unnecessarily and pressing on to the finish—who eventually finds himself, in spite of all his troubles and difficulties, accomplishing his task.

VIII

ORGANIZING FOR RECORD-BREAKING ATTEMPTS

THERE is no sport I know of at which the breaking of records is easily accomplished. Motor-racing is certainly no exception. Although the actual period occupied in making an attack on a record may be a matter of minutes, even of seconds, yet the preparation needed for this effort—this tiny flash in time—may well have taken years of planning, hard work and the expenditure of considerable sums of money.

Consider what is required in the undertaking of a record-breaking attempt. The three main essentials are the machine itself, the course or track over which it is to be driven, and the driver. All three have to be as near perfection as possible. The smallest defect may mean that vital difference between success and failure. There is no room at all for the second-best.

The development of the racing-car has been little short of miraculous. In 1899 the fastest race ever run had been won at 30 m.p.h. with a 6-h.p. car. The next year a 28-h.p. car won at 40 m.p.h. over a distance of more than 800 miles. Twelve months afterwards a 60-h.p. car won a 300-mile race at 53 m.p.h. In early 1903 a 70-h.p. machine showed a race-winning speed of 65 m.p.h., and in 1904 a 90-h.p. car set up 72 m.p.h. in a 225-mile event. Thus from the 6-h.p. machine of 1899 the horse-power fairly leaped year by year: 28 h.p.—60 h.p.—70 h.p.—90 h.p. Within the next couple of years manufacturers were building machines of 120 h.p., as is shown by the De Dietrich which won a race in 1906.

This progress both in power and speed resulted mainly from bigger and more powerful engines. The pioneer inventors had to feel their way towards efficient engines, and the striking developments I have just quoted shows how very rapidly they progressed. Because their first efforts were crude it would be wrong to come to the conclusion that they were not clever men. It is almost certain that in another fifty years many of the things we do to-day will appear primitive. Actually, the pioneers in motor-design were exceedingly acute men, but they had to make those first weak little engines in order to find what problems had to be attacked.

In those early days engines used to overheat. This brought the idea of providing them with water jackets in order to keep them cool. Next, they found the water boiled. This brought tubes exposed to the air through which the water could circulate: the modern radiator, in fact.

It is possible to trace the whole growth of cars from the first principles employed by the pioneers —principles which were all the time being improved upon through practical test and experience. When the designers of earlier days found that their engines worked well, they then set about increasing the power. The first motor-car of all had only ¾ h.p. It could travel at about 8 m.p.h. when moving flat out; it had spindly wheels and narrow, solid tyres, and its power was much too low to cope with the indifferent roads of 1884. The same trouble was found when other cars followed, although it was partly overcome by the fitting of engines with bigger cylinders, which gave off about 4 h.p. This, however, was still not enough, and it was then that some designer had the bright idea of coupling together two single-cylinder engines of 4 h.p. and working them on the same crankshaft. This scheme provided an 8-h.p. engine. The next step in progress came with four-cylinder power-units.. But this progress was not bought cheaply, for each step forward only resulted from the overcoming of many snags and difficulties.

Engines kept on growing bigger. Some had cylinders like chimney-pots, six inches and more in diameter and very deep, using great quantities of petrol. They were evolved directly from the primitive, early cars, and were themselves primitive, because they were quite unrefined.

There came a time when designers realized that a halt must be called to increasing the engine-size. Engines had become so large and heavy that quite a percentage of their power had to be utilized merely in pulling their own weight. As far as racing was concerned this was most unsatisfactory, and so we see now the designing of lighter and smaller engines, but they were not less powerful. This really was the birth of engine-design as contrasted with the actual building of engines. Development became scientific, and the evolution of the modern motor-car began.

These new designs created fresh difficulties. Apart from problems concerning the efficiency of the engines, attention was now turned to the whole chassis. It had to be made lighter, and yet remain just as strong, because these new cars were no slower; it was this which turned attention to streamlining, and some attempts were made to lessen wind resistance by the building of low, smooth bodies.

A great spurt forward in motor-engineering design resulted from experience gained in the First World War. This has also been the case from knowledge learned in the last war. Designers of aero engines quickly discovered that the principles used in the building of racing motor-cars were equally applicable in their own work. In an aeroplane engine what is termed the "power-weight ratio" is of the utmost importance. This simply means the ratio of an engine's power to its weight. For example, consider two different engines both having the same weight, say 100 pounds. One engine, however, gives off 50 h.p., while the other engine gives off 25 h.p. The first engine provides double the horse-power for the same weight.

The power-weight ratio of the first engine is two pounds for 1 h.p., while for the second it is four pounds for 1 h.p.

The Rolls-Royce engine used in *Blue Bird* for my 301-m.p.h. record on Bonneville Salt Flats, in 1935, weighed 1,780 pounds and gave off 2,500 horse-power—roughly one pound of engine-weight per 1½ h.p. Since then still greater advances have been made.

The present-day racing-car is, of course, specially designed for the purpose. Its manufacture involves endless tests and costly experiments. A small improvement here, a tiny change there, may easily add a few miles' extra speed to its final performance. So many things seem to go wrong, but it is a very strange thing that the more trouble a car gives during practice—within reason, of course—the better chance it has on the day it sets out to beat a record. Many a time men have had to work all night on a car, and have made it ready for the start only during the last hour, for the machine to run perfectly and gain its laurels. Conversely, there are times when everything goes wrong all the time. It does seem, however, that a car which proves recalcitrant is merely overcoming all its troubles before the great day, instead of saving them up until the event is being run off.

There is, I often think, a considerable resemblance between a racing-car and a thoroughbred racehorse. Both have to be handled carefully and considerately. The machine is a very highly tuned piece of mechanism which must not be abused if the best results are to be attained. It must be driven not only with intelligence but even with affection. The ideal combination is when man and machine become almost a unity.

Two wars, whatever else they did, certainly brought great advances to our knowledge of motor-design. Perhaps the most important advance has been in the use of new metals. So often designers are far ahead in theory to what can be carried out in practice. This is where new metals help to turn the dream into reality.

Special metals are invariably costly. A designer may feel that some new metal will greatly increase the efficiency of the racing-car he is planning, but the cost is prohibitive. In war this is not a barrier to development, and the result is that the costly and usually lengthy essential experiments are carried out by the state, resulting in a product which later comes to be available to commercial industry. This same matter of research applies to experiments with fuels, often again resulting in increased engine-efficiency.

High speed makes sound tyres vitally necessary; it is the research work of men engaged in the production of tyres, their efforts to produce something which would stand up to the strain of high speeds, that has helped materially in the development of present-day speed records. Even this progress, however, has only come about by risk and trial.

I have already described how the Dunlop Company, following the tragic disaster that occurred at Fanoe during my attempt on the speed record, experimented until they found a much more efficient tyre—the forerunner, indeed, of what every motorist uses to-day.

Once the pioneers had their cars showing any speed at all, they began to try to find out just how fast they would go. They did this by the simple process of measuring a length of road and putting their machines through it under full throttle. The same principle applies to-day. There are speed records for every class of car, from machines with small engines to cars with power-units as big as anything that men have been able to build into a chassis frame. The pace of cars with defined engine size is always interesting, and some remarkable records have been achieved,[1] but still greater interest lies in the question of just how fast a man can travel in a car: in other words, to what figure the absolute record for land speed can be pushed.

Racing men had known for years that smooth stretches of sand were ideal for speed. Even if the surface were a little yielding the pace of the car itself made this of no moment; one can skate fast

[1] There are approximately a thousand officially recognized world's records, international class records, compression ignition class records and British records. The world's records embrace many long-distance performances, including a distance of 185,353 miles covered in 133 days —or over seven times round the earth at the Equator.

over thin ice which would break if one simply stood on it, and driving over certain sands is analogous. There is a proviso, however, that the harder the sand the better the surface it presents to the car, and the greater the possible speed, always assuming the sand to be smooth.

As speeds have increased so has it become harder to find suitable sand tracks over which a car can compete for a record. The chosen track must provide sufficient distance to accelerate and decelerate before and after the measured mile. At least twelve miles is needed to accomplish this, and a greater length is in fact to be preferred. The surface of the track must be absolutely smooth. Record breaking at high speed is largely a matter of gaining mere fractions of time. The least deviation from a straight course, wheel-slip, faint ripples on the sand—any one of a number of almost infinitesimal factors can rob the machine of success.

Everything is so enormously magnified. A hummock of sand only an inch in height and practically unobservable to the naked eye can send a car off the beach in a great jump, perhaps thirty feet in length. With each second gained in speed, still greater demands are made upon the car, and the driver's system is still more put under stress. On a rough track it requires every bit of strength to hold the wheel which kicks under one's hands and blisters the palms. It also plays havoc with the tyres, and the toughest tyres can be literally torn to shreds.

When it comes to the actual selection of a suitable race-track over which to make a modern high-speed record the choice is extremely limited. Length of track and a suitable surface, visibility, altitude, accessibility and quite a number of other factors have to be considered. In Britain there is certainly no suitable stretch capable of allowing modern cars to go full out. When I made my successful attempt on the 150 m.p.h. record it was at Pendine Sands on the west coast of Wales. Pendine is a lonely desolate spot, a long stretch of sand, out of the usual tourist area, visited by few. It was about the only stretch of sand in Britain suitable, but is now obsolete. It is not nearly long enough to give the high-speed cars of to-day sufficient space in which to accelerate and decelerate before and after the measured mile.

The Redcar and Saltburn sands on the Yorkshire coast were considered for a while by those who were anxious to find a British speed track, but they had to be ruled out. I certainly regard the Saltburn sands as the best for racing in this country, even though there is not a sufficiently long stretch to permit of a record-breaking attempt. I did set up a record of 135 m.p.h. on a twelve-cylinder Sunbeam on these sands in 1922, but this was done within a space of five miles.

The bars that prevent this stretch of the Yorkshire sands from being turned into the finest speed track in Europe are the piers at Redcar and Saltburn and the fact that it is not dead straight. To get up really high speeds, a motorist would have to steer his car between the supporting piles of the two piers at a speed of hundreds of miles an hour. This is not feasible, or at best is highly dangerous. If those piers could be demolished . . . .

In my own search for the perfect track I have gone far afield. There was the Syrian Desert, for instance, which I once considered. One day, perhaps, it will prove to be a world's speed track. There are enormous stretches of sun-baked mud pans, dead smooth in some places, but most uneven and overgrown with camelthorn in others. There is a stretch west of Rutba, where there is nearly 300 miles of hard, smooth going. I realized that there were certain snags, however. There might be trouble with mirages, and also with the Druse tribesmen who inhabit the area. They are good marksmen and love a moving target! The mirages are so bad that any speed attempt, and all practice runs, would have to be made before eight o'clock in the morning. After that hour the mirages blot out the field of vision and give the driver the impression that he is about to go over the edge of a cliff during the summer months.

Another danger is broken beer-bottles! European travellers by motor-coach and car, and tribesmen who have imbibed the spirit of our civilization, are both equally in the habit of casting their empty bottles light-heartedly away. One other drawback in the summer is the whirling black pillars of dust, sometimes 200 feet high, which move across the face of the desert like waterspouts at sea.

Brief mention should be made of Fanoe where I made an attempt on the record. This is an island, which is opposite Esjberg, on the Danish coast. The island is long and narrow, and it had a course some six miles in length marked out over firm sand. At the present day it is quite unsuitable.

The Sahara is another part of the world where I once sought out the perfect speed track. I had been told of a suitable site north-west of Timbuktu, and decided to fly there to inspect it. On the way I looked at various possibilities. It was clear, however, that the Sahara would never do. Not only were possible spots highly inaccessible, but, as in the Syrian desert, there were the constant mirages, islands, lakes, sea beaches and groves of trees, which appeared and disappeared like nightmares. Obviously it would be utterly hopeless to attempt to drive a car at high speed in such a place, where at one moment one would appear to be charging a mountain, the next to be plunging into the sea.

I had flown out to make this Saharan survey in a Gypsy Moth, accompanied by Squadron-Leader Don, an old friend. On our return trip we ran into a series of unpleasant adventures from which we were lucky to escape alive.

We had reached Oran, the Algerian port, in safety, and from there intended to follow the shore line, recrossing the Mediterranean at Gibraltar. Before leaving we were warned that a certain stretch of the coast was exceedingly dangerous, because of the presence of hostile Riff tribesmen. At this point the mountains were particularly rugged and came sheer down to the sea, forming great cliffs which made any sort of landing impossible; in any case, this was the one stretch of coast in which it was highly desirable not to try even to descend.

We left Oran and had about two hours in the air when we found ourselves level with the territory against which we had been warned. Shortly afterwards, when we were 1,500 feet up and about a mile out to sea, there came a blow-back from the engine, followed by such vibration that it seemed as if the power-unit would shake itself loose; an inlet valve had jammed, and it was only by good fortune that fire did not follow.

With the engine dead, the machine was turned towards the coast, while Don and I searched anxiously for a landing place. We saw nothing but rocks and steep cliffs until—with the plane now very low—we cleared a headland and, beyond this, discovered a small bay with a narrow, shingle beach. It was the only possible landing place, and the craft came down just on the edge of the beach, hit a huge boulder and plunged into the sea.

We climbed out of the machine, landing up to our necks in water, but grabbing the tail of the machine. We did not want to lose our one chance of escape from this most inhospitable country, while there was a possibility that, if we got the plane clear of the water, we might be able to make a repair and find some way of taking off again.

Although there was not a soul in sight when we landed, nevertheless we had been floundering in the sea for only two or three minutes when some forty or fifty outlandish-looking Riffs appeared on the beach. Knowing about some of their practices with prisoners I felt very much between the devil and the deep sea. However, we shouted to them for help. They did not understand, but they came and hauled the plane safely on to the little beach.

They were a bearded, dirty, evil-smelling lot, and it was only because they thought we were Spanish airmen that they did not take us prisoner; they were afraid that, if they mishandled us, Spanish bombers might arrive later on a punitive expedition.

The gift of some five-peseta pieces which I happened to possess eventually caused the Riffs to disappear, but it left us in an awkward situation. The nearest town was Tetuan, seventy miles distant, and the country in between is most inhospitable. All we had with us for refreshment was a small bottle of Vichy water, a flask of brandy, and two packets of chocolate.

We decided to set out for Tetuan. The going was terribly rough, most of the time being spent in clambering over cliffs, and we often found our way barred by jutting cliffs, around which we were obliged to swim. We carried on, but without much hope of getting through.

When darkness fell we turned inland a little, and

then we heard dogs yapping in the gloom and realized that we had reached some kind of village. It was now past midnight. As we stood there a giant of a man appeared and proved to be friendly. He was the local chief, and he offered us food and water, but both were so nauseous that we had to leave them alone. We did get some sleep, however.

The next morning we resumed our tramp along the difficult coast, growing less and less hopeful of reaching civilization as the hours passed. A burning sun blazed down on us all the time. Then, I slipped on a rough slope and injured my leg badly. I thought I should be unable to go on and begged Don to go on, but he insisted on staying with me. After a time I managed to limp along in great pain.

We had had nothing to drink since leaving Oran thirty hours before, and the Vichy water we now decided to drink only made our thirst more intense. We came to great stretches of rusted barbed wire, marking an area over which fighting between the Riffs and Spaniards had recently taken place. We scratched and tore ourselves in getting through these defences.

Our shoes had given out and we were now at our last gasp. It seemed impossible that we could go any further. We dozed for some time under the shadow of some rocks. I roused after a while, and when I sat up almost the first thing I saw was the silhouette of a man on a ridge—fully four miles away. I saw that he wore trousers, indicating that he was not one of the Riffs but a European.

Excitedly Don and I started forward, eventually coming up to the man and discovering that he formed part of a Spanish outpost. We were taken to the commandant and received excellent treatment. The next day we were taken to Ceuta. A guard was sent down to look after the plane, and the Spanish authorities followed this with a cruiser and a lighter. The plane was loaded on the lighter and brought back to Ceuta, being shipped across to British territory at Gibraltar.

When we returned to England, we found that the story of our unexpected adventures had received a good deal of attention, and news of our search for a high-speed course reached South Africa. A few weeks later, I was told of a dry lake which was called Verneuk Pan. There was a Dr. Martin who lived in the little village of Brandvlei, about fifty miles from the lake. He saw the notice about our search and wrote to the *Cape Times*, suggesting that someone should inspect Verneuk Pan. He said that the lake-bed offered a stretch of level, hard surface, twenty miles long, and ten miles wide.

An assistant editor from the *Cape Times* went to the Pan, and reported on its suitability. I received full particulars and sent out a representative to secure more details. As a result of his report I decided to take *Blue Bird* to South Africa, and try to break the record there.

Another suggested speed-track which I once considered was the Ninety Mile Beach in New Zealand. This beach lies about 250 miles north of Auckland, and it includes a dead-level perfectly straight stretch of some seventeen miles, which, according to all reports, was ideal for high speeds. The spot is desolate, and it would have been necessary to have formed a camp on the shore, but it appeared to hold advantages over Daytona—and many disadvantages as well. It was a very long way from England, and a month would be occupied in reaching it, while Daytona was hardly more than a week away, and here the American authorities had everything available and thoroughly organized. In the end I decided to go to this place for my next attempt on the speed record.

When I made my first visit to Daytona my initial impressions were disappointing; the weather was cold, the sea was rough, and the sand was very uneven.

Its entire length is not available for record attempts, because a pier cuts the beach in two. The course is set south of this and only a stretch of ten miles is available. At the north end the pier limits the course and at the south the Halifax River bends round the sea.

Although Daytona had been used on several occasions by drivers attempting world-speed records, it has a number of defects. It is a very expensive place to stay at. The man who goes there to break a record will find that it will cost him a great deal of money, and, to crown the total, there is a charge of just on £700 for the transport of the car from New York to Daytona and back.

Further defects in this course include the fact that the beach is very sensitive to weather conditions, demanding a wind from the north-east before it can be left really smooth. If the wind is in the wrong quarter, the sand becomes rough and lumpy, and sometimes strewn with shells. The days of waiting for perfect track conditions are a great strain, and it is obvious that no one could ever be certain of when the sands would be in a safe state for the very high rates of speed attained.

Sometimes when the beach is in good condition the visibility is bad. The atmosphere is hazy, and there are sea mists. Both these defects affect speed. High winds are yet another difficulty. All this variety of considerations cause anxiety, and experience has made it clear that this beach is not safe to cope with present-day high speed.

Wheel-spin on this course often brought fantastic results. I have seen my car recording 328 m.p.h., but the actual speed, owing to wheel-spin, only came to 273 m.p.h.

Undoubtedly the finest and fastest track in the world which is reasonably accessible is the Bonneville Salt Flats. This is the only place I know of where modern high speeds are feasible. It has its defects, of course, the main one being its somewhat isolated position in an arid and deserted region of Utah. Another disadvantage is its altitude (4,200 feet), for this means that an engine loses nineteen per cent of its brake horse-power, but, on the other hand, there is a compensating gain of fourteen per cent by lessened wind resistance. The great desert heat is also trying. It is so hot there that awnings have to be erected at each end of the course to keep the car as cool as possible whilst wheels are being changed.

Its great advantage is the ample space available.

There is all the "sea-room" one could wish for. No matter how difficult the driver's position may be by reason of mechanical failure, it is hardly likely to become desperate. This is a valuable asset.

One interesting sensation I experienced when travelling over this huge salt pan was that one could see that the world was round: the distant edge of horizon and earth's surface kept on extending and extending as I raced over the ground at 300 m.p.h.

IX

THE FUTURE OF SPEED ON WHEELS

WHAT DOES the future hold in respect of speed records on land?

This is not an easy question to answer, for the accurate forecasting of future events is one of the most difficult things to accomplish; and motor-car speeds are no exception. In just over fifty years speed on wheels has risen from about 17 m.p.h. attained by the winning car in the first Paris-Rouen race, to over 400 m.p.h. Almost as remarkable as the astounding rise in speed has been the complete change in the outlook of people regarding future possibilities. In the early days not even the most enthusiastic motorist would have imagined that our present record speeds could be attained; at best it would have just been a wild, idle dream, and yet this dream has come true—within a life's span.

To-day we live in the age of the machine. The science of mechanism, the development of the human mind and brain in combating the laws of nature, have altogether largely conquered the stupendous forces which sway and affect the lives of all inhabitants of the globe. They have also affected our imaginative outlook. Fifty years ago speed was regarded by most people as being a blasphemy, something they hated; and they felt very strongly about the efforts the few pioneers were making to develop it. But now few people get angry about speed, for nothing seems to be potentially impossible. We have become mentally numbed by the soulless and subservient mechanism which is the power of to-day and of the future. We have already forgotten, except in a historical sense, the conditions under which our forefathers lived. Thus we find it difficult to understand and appreciate the measure and immensity of the influence on our everyday life of the science of mechanism.

Now we have just arrived on the threshold of atomic power with all its possibilities. What effect will this epoch-making invention have on our lives, and on speed—say, in fifty years' time? I would certainly not care to hazard a guess, for it is absolutely unpredictable.

When, therefore, I write about the future of speed I must confine myself to what I think may be attained during the next few years. It certainly seems to me that it may be *possible* for man to travel on land at 500 m.p.h. I wish to emphasize the word "possible", for before such a speed can be attained, or even at 450 m.p.h., certain problems will have to be solved and overcome, as undoubtedly they will be.

At the present time the possibilities of the petrol-driven speed-car have nearly reached their limits; the gas-turbine or jet-engine has taken its place. Then, the development of atomic power for commercial purposes and not merely for destruction is obviously going to be a vital factor that must enter into the raising of land speeds in the future. Let me make it clear that the petrol-driven car is not going to be out-of-date for ordinary commercial purposes. It is obvious that on roads motorists are hardly likely to be allowed to drive at really high speeds. There must always be speed limits. So that even if a jet-propelled car was to achieve a speed of 500 m.p.h., it would not permit the ordinary driver to travel even at 5 m.p.h. faster. Anyhow, as far as jet engines are concerned, their present fuel consumption is so great and expensive that they cannot be regarded as economic for the purposes of commercial transportation. Their value lies in power for extra speed, whatever the cost: on fighter-planes, for example.

There are many advantages to be obtained by a racing-car driven by a jet engine. The car to start with is of considerably less weight, for there is neither transmission, gear-box, nor clutch. Then, this type of car is fairly easy to produce and is comparatively simple in design. On the other hand there are certain difficulties and problems to be faced. The main one being how to keep the car itself on the ground when it is travelling at really high speeds.

When a car is travelling at a very high speed, say 400 m.p.h., wind tends to pile up under it, and raises or lifts it into the air. It becomes, in fact, air-borne. This is a condition that I have myself had to face in my latter attempts on the record. No car leaving the ground in this way can have its speed officially recorded. All its wheels must adhere to the earth's surface.

The difficulty of keeping the car on the ground is mainly an aerodynamical problem, and its solution lies largely in work carried out by scientists in wind-tunnels. The use of airfoils would probably help to give the downward pressure needed to keep the car on the ground. Steering is another difficulty at very high speeds, and there must be improvements made in this direction also. The question of suitable tyres has in the past often been a limiting factor, but the tyre companies have invariably found a solution.

Another problem to be faced will be to find a track suitable for the speeds which may be reached. This is a difficulty which has occurred often in the past. Pendine, Fanoe, Daytona—all had to be given up as the speed record rose. At Bonneville Salt Flats, which is at present the most suitable track, the longest stretch available is fifteen miles. This is just sufficient to cope with a car travelling at 400 m.p.h. A car travelling at 450 m.p.h. or 500 m.p.h. would certainly require a longer track unless the car can be built much lighter than heretofore.

Perhaps the biggest barrier to the attainment of great land speeds will be the question of cost. In the past most attempts at breaking the record have been financed largely by the person concerned. As the speed rose the cost did likewise. It has now reached a stage when any further attempt on the record is likely to require a huge sum of money—perhaps £30,000. And in return there is little return except national prestige. No longer can private individuals afford such an expenditure, and it is extremely doubtful whether private concerns will be interested.

My conclusion, therefore, is that while speeds of 450 and 500 m.p.h. are possible on land, they are not likely to be attained because of this problem of cost.

THE WORLD'S LAND-SPEED RECORD

DATE	DRIVER	CAR	SPEED M.P.H.
1898	Chasseloup-Laubat	Jeantaud	39·24
1899	Jenatzy	Jenatzy	41·42
1899	Chasseloup-Laubat	Jeantaud	43·69
1899	Jenatzy	Jenatzy	49·42
1899	Chasseloup-Laubat	Jeantaud	58·25
1899	Jenatzy	Jenatzy	65·82
1902	Serpollet	Serpollet	75·06
1902	Vanderbilt	Mors	76·08
1902	Fournier	Mors	76·60
1902	Augieres	Mors	77·13
1903	Duray	Gobron-Brillié	84·21
1903	Ford	Ford	91·37
1904	Vanderbilt	Mercédès	92·30
1904	Rigolly	Gobron-Brillié	93·20
1904	de Caters	Mercédès	97·26
1904	Rigolly	Gobron-Brillié	103·56
1904	Barras	Darracq	104·53
1905	Hemery	Darracq	109·65
1905	Bowden	Mercédès	109·75
1906	Marriott	Stanley	121·57
1909	Hemery	Benz	125·90
1910	Oldfield	Benz	131·72
1911	Burman	Benz	141·73
1919	de Palma	Packard	149·87
1920	Milton	Duesenberg	156·04
1922	Guinness	Sunbeam	129·17
1924	Thomas	Leyland-Thomas	129·73
1924	Eldridge	Fiat	145·90
1924	R. Thomas	Delage	143·31
1925	Campbell	Sunbeam	150·86
1926	Segrave	Sunbeam	152·33
1926	Thomas	Higham	169·23
1926	Thomas	Higham	171·09
1927	Campbell	Napier-Campbell	174·88
1927	Segrave	Sunbeam	203·79
1928	Campbell	Napier-Campbell	206·95
1928	Keech	Ehite-Triplex	207·55
1929	Segrave	Irving-Special	231·44
1931	Campbell	Napier-Campbell	246·09
1932	Campbell	Napier-Campbell	253·97
1933	Campbell	Rolls-Royce-Campbell	272·46
1935	Campbell	Rolls-Royce-Campbell	276·82
1935	Campbell	Rolls-Royce-Campbell	301·13
1937	Eyston	Thunderbolt	312·0
1938	Eyston	Thunderbolt	345·50
1938	Cobb	Railton	350·20
1938	Eyston	Thunderbolt	357·50
1939	Cobb	Railton	369·70
1947	Cobb	Railton	394·20

INDEX